Reviews of *Starting a Micro Business*

When my son started his teen business—which he eventually sold in a million dollar deal—he had little knowledge about how to structure it and handle the tax side. It was Carol Topp who helped him learn how to set up his business, keep records, and plan for future growth. Chris S., Madeira, Ohio

Carol Topp's books not only helped me launch a successful micro business, but gave me the ability to run my business in an organized, professional manner. She has a simple, instructive, helpful writing style that is easy to understand and execute. The books have helped me accomplish one of the greatest goal I could ever achieve. Jade B., age 16

The book was amazing! With it I am making double minimum wage and I'm not even old enough to work at McDonald's or Kroger! The book has taught me that I don't have to be 15 to have a job! *Starting a Micro Business* has taught me how to manage my time and money wisely between my business, school, and other activities. Ethan E., age 14

Starting a Micro Business is the first business planning resource that I have seen that is geared specifically for teens who are thinking of starting a business. It is a great resource to help a teenager learn about business and to ultimately start their own business. I strongly recommend this book and its very practical, doable approach to any aspiring young entrepreneur. I think it provides teens a great first step into the entrepreneurial world. Michael P. Licata, Ph.D, Accounting Professor, Villanova University

Running a Micro Business

by

Carol Topp, CPA

Ambassador Publishing
Cincinnati, Ohio

ISBN 978-0-9829245-1-8

Scripture taken from THE HOLY BIBLE, NEW INTERNATIONAL VER-
SION® Copyright © 1973, 1978, 1984 International Bible Society.
Used by permission of Zondervan.

Cover Design: Dave Huff
Author Photo: Cathy Lyons

Disclaimer and Limitation of Liability
This book is designed to provide accurate and authoritative information about the subject matter covered. The author is not rendering
legal, accounting, or other professional advice.

The fact that a company, organization or website is mentioned does
not mean that the author endorses the information or services provided. The resources mentioned in this book should be evaluated by the
reader. Readers should also be aware that organizations and web
sites mentioned may have been changed or ceased operations since
the publication of this book.

Any tax advice contained in this book was not intended or written to be
used, and cannot be used, by any taxpayer for the purpose of avoiding
penalties that may be imposed under the Internal Revenue Code or
applicable state or local tax law provisions. Furthermore, this book
was not intended or written to support the promotion or marketing of
any of the transactions or matters it may address.

This book is dedicated

to my family: Dave, Emily and Sarah,

to my teenage micro business clients,

Phillip, Lucas, Emily, Matthew, Lauren, Meghan,

and many more,

to Amanda Bennett,

who encouraged me from the start,

to all the homeschool families

who told me they wanted this book,

and to the Lord.

Table of Contents

Introduction
What's Different About
This Book?

I wrote this book because I knew that teenagers needed it. As a mother of two teenagers, I have met plenty of students that wanted to make some money, but didn't know how to get started. I also met a few ambitious students who did make serious money by creating websites and mowing grass, but they needed help with business issues. I started searching for books to help these teenagers.

I didn't like what I found.

There are plenty of books for kids who want to start a business like a lemonade stand. They are geared toward children who are just playing at running a business. They are usually cute books that explain the difference between quarters and dollars and how a bank is a safe place to put your money.

That's necessary information for children, but teenagers need more.

There are plenty of books for people wanting to be entrepreneurs. They are usually geared toward young adults just out of college. The assumption in these books is that the reader can get a bank loan (most teenagers cannot) or that the reader has plenty of time to devote to starting a business.

These books do not consider that a teenager needs to do homework, eat, sleep, and still have a social life.

Finally, I ran across a few (but very few) books for teenage entrepreneurs. Some were books written for adults that were repackaged for teenagers by substituting a few words here and there. They were full of unrealistic ideas. I found one book that recommended a teenager open a restaurant! As if a teenager has the time (or money) to run a restaurant! Other books were full of inspiring stories about teen entrepreneurs, but they left me feeling intimidated because the teenagers featured were so very successful.

Their stories seemed beyond the grasp of a normal American teenager.

Some of the information in these books was useful, but they were inadequate in many areas. Few covered business plans. Even fewer discussed taxes in an intelligent and helpful way. There were rarely examples of how to keep good records and very few real life examples.

So I wrote this book because I knew that teenagers needed it.

This book is geared toward teenagers and their lives. There are no unrealistic expectations of opening a restaurant. There are ideas of businesses that real teenagers have started and run successfully. I provide a lot of examples of teenagers I know personally. I walk you through some very important topics such as making a plan and avoiding debt.

That's how this book is different!

Carol Topp, CPA
Author

> This book is very practical. If you want inspiration, it's here in small bites, but primarily this book will be helpful and useful to you. Think of it as getting a CPA's advice for under $20.00!

Chapter One
Sales

Marianne wanted to earn some money by selling Mary Kay makeup, "I am not a sales person. I don't want to do any selling," she told me. I was uncertain about Marianne's future success, because selling is vital in running a micro business. Marianne sold cosmetics for two years and then quit. Although she had a good product that she believed in, her failure to gain customers caused her micro business to fold.

Selling a product or service may not be easy. You need to believe in the product you are selling. You may need to overcome shyness, fear, or rejection. Selling can be hard work, but if you know your product can benefit people, then you will want to tell them about it. In this chapter, you will learn how to present your product or service to your customers in an appealing way. Start with an attention-getting statement.

Your Sales Statement

***We don't want to push our ideas on to customers,
we simply want to make what they want.***
Laura Ashley, fashion designer

Customers do not buy your product or service just to give you money. They have a need, and somehow, you are meeting that need. Customers buy something because they want to feel good, look better, have fun, or save time or money. Your product or service should benefit your customers in some way.

Create a sales statement for your product or service that emphasizes the main benefits to the customer.

A sales statement should be very short, five to seven words at most, and convey a benefit or action you want the customer to take, such as "Buy my doggie treats now for a happy puppy." Using a twist on words or a rhyme can be catchy. "Max mows your grass, so you can relax." Keep it short, simple, and memorable.

A sales statement is sometimes called a tag line and is usually placed after your name or business name on advertising material. Print your tag line on your advertising fliers and business cards. Use it when explaining your business or making a sales presentation.

Selling in Person

Selling techniques can be very different depending on whether you meet your customers in person or sell on-line. You may use different techniques and tools. Many teenage micro business owners sell only to a local market, where they meet their customers face-to-face. These business owners will probably use a verbal sales presentation and order forms. On-line sales are more dependent on building trust, having a great website, and an easy ordering system.

Your Sales Presentation

To satisfy our customers' needs, we'll give them what they want, not what we want to give them.
Steve James, author

If you meet your customers in person, you should have a short sales presentation prepared describing your product or service. A sales presentation is a bit like a live TV commercial, except you deliver it in person to potential customers. It can be quite short—as little as 30 seconds—but no more than two minutes. The components of a good sales presentation include:

1. Introducing yourself and your business name
2. A description of your main product or service
3. Two or three of the main benefits of the product or service
4. A brief demonstration, sample, or picture, if possible
5. Your sales statement or tag line
6. Your price
7. How to reach you or order
8. A call to action

Example of a Sales Presentation
Adam trains children to be Jedi knights at birthday parties. His attention-getting tag line is "Do you dream of becoming a Jedi knight?"

I'm Adam (name) and I visit children's birthday parties (business) as Jedi Master, Adaro Moced. I can train your child and his friends in light saber fighting (main benefit). It is perfectly safe, because I use Styrofoam pool "noodles" as light sabers (second benefit). Let me demonstrate (demonstration). I'm available for birthday parties where I come in costume and offer games, stories, demonstrations, and dueling practice. Here's a brochure describing my prices and how to contact me (price and contact information). Does your child dream of becoming a Jedi knight? (tag line) Give me a call (call to action).

A sales presentation can be used at a trade fair or craft show, if that is how you sell your products. It can be recorded as a video for your website. It can be written for use on your website, flier, or advertisements. Some teenage micro business owners go door-to-door in their neighborhood and use their sales pitch on neighbors. There are many ways to use a short sales presentation, so tailor your presentation to your customers and your business.

Making the Sale

Many sales are lost because the salesperson never asks the customer to buy. That seems unbelievable, but it is true. A business owner can spend a lot of time creating a sales presentation and marketing material, but never bring the customer to the point of actually making a purchase. There are several techniques you can use to move from a sales pitch to completing a sale including asking questions and using forms.

Ask Leading Questions

After you have explained your product or service, it is time to ask the customer to buy. There are dozens of ways to do this.

- When is a good time for me to _____(offer your service)?
- Would you prefer _____ or _____(you show different products)?
- What is the best day to _____(offer your service)?
- When would you like me to start?
- How many _____ do you need?
- Would you like to see a price list?
- Can I get you an order form?
- What questions can I answer?
- Would you like me to do _____ next?

Use an Order Form

Many salespeople like to use a paper form such as a price list, order form, or registration form to make a sale. These forms show you are a legitimate business and give the customer information on what you offer. It can also be a reminder if they chose not to buy from you today.

The order form should have your name and contact information as well as a place for the customer to fill in their name and contact information. The center section of an order form usually lists the items ordered and a column for the quantity and price. At the bottom is usually a place to total the purchase and add sales tax if necessary. Many order forms come in duplicate form, so you can give a copy to the customer and keep a copy for yourself.

A price list can be included on the order form at the top or bottom. If you have many products, a separate price list might be needed.

They Do Not Seem Interested

Advertisers tell us that it can take ten impressions before a consumer buys a product, so be prepared for customers who may seem uncertain. Customers may not buy from you for a lot of reasons. Perhaps they do not need what you are selling, the price is too high, they are not ready to buy or they do not trust you enough. You cannot always control your customers' buying decisions, but you can be gently persistent by asking a few questions.

- Ask if you could give a demonstration or a sample. Say "Would you like to see how this works?" or "Would you like to taste a sample?"
- Provide additional information by asking, "Do you have any questions?"
- Ask if they would like a flier, brochure, or price list. Try to leave something in their hands.
- Ask if they have a friend or neighbor who could use your service.

Always be polite and thank them for their time or for listening to you, even if they say no. They will remember your politeness and may contact you in the future.

Getting Paid in Person

There are several techniques to use to get paid, including making statements or using forms. Signal your customers that it is time to pay by saying one of the following:

> "I've finished ___, would you like to see it before you write me a check?"

> "Is there anything else you need before I total up your bill?"

> "I'll make up your receipt now."

> "Your total comes to ___. Will you be paying in cash or by check?"

> "Here's your invoice. I'm happy to wait while you get your checkbook."

> "Will you be paying today or would you like me to send you an invoice?" Do not use this statement with a new customer. Only let previous customers who have paid you promptly delay their payments.

Use Business Forms To Get Paid
Handing a paper to a customer is a good signal that it is time to pay. There are at least three types of forms you can use:

1. A bill. This is handed to the customer at the time of service or sale.

2. A statement. This is a summary of all the charges a customer has accumulated over time. It is frequency used by music teachers that collect payments once a month instead of every week. Statements can be emailed or delivered on paper.

For many years, my daughter's piano teacher used a brightly colored sticky note with the amount I owed her as a statement. She stuck it onto Sarah's piano books as a reminder to pay her. Other piano teachers have mailed or emailed statements to me every month.

3. An invoice. This form lists the services you have already provided or products you delivered, but allow the customer to pay at a later date. Only allow returning customers to pay you later. Do not allow a new customer to delay their payment, because you may never get paid.

What To Do If Customers Do Not Pay

Most of your clients will pay when you hand them a bill, but sometimes they forget or do not have a checkbook with them. In those cases you need to remind them.

- Send another copy of the bill, statement, or invoice. Email is a good reminder or use regular mail if you must. This usually does the trick. Most people are forgetful and not out to cheat you.

- Call the customer and ask if they received your bill.

- Explain to late paying customers that your policy is to charge a late fee for bills that are past due. Suggest that they can avoid late fees by getting your payment to you by the end of the week.

- If a customer is late paying you, do not do any additional services for them.

I usually get paid by check when I give my tax clients their tax return. In one case, a new client did not bring a checkbook or enough cash to pay me. I gave him the tax return because he promised he would send me a check. He never did, even after I emailed and called him several times. Now, I do not hand over a tax return to a new client until he or she has paid.

Payment Policies

After you've been running your business for a while, you will come up with some payment policies that work well for you. A few common payment policies include:

- Ask for some money up-front as a down payment. This is a common practice if you will be doing a large job for a customer. It is very common to ask for a small amount, perhaps 10-20% of the total price before you begin work.

- Progress payments. Ask for payments as you do each part of a large job. For example, I asked my graphic designer to do five tasks for me. He billed me after three tasks were complete and then again when the job was finished.

- Charge a late fee for customers who are more than 30 days late in paying you. Your late fee can be a percentage of the total cost (5-10% is customary) or a flat fee such as $10.

- Have a policy regarding bounced checks. If a customer pays you with a bad check, your bank may fine *you* when the check is deposited. It may not seem fair, but it is a common practice. You, in turn, should charge the customer at least a $10 fee to cover your bank fees. Some stores charge as much as $25 for a bounced check.

- Consider marking up your price to accept Paypal or credit card payments. Paypal and credit card companies typically take 2-4% of the payment as their fee. Most business owners usually consider these fees as part of doing business, so make sure you take the fees into consideration when pricing your products or services.

Selling On-line

Many techniques of selling in person can be used on-line as well, especially a tag line and a sales presentation. Consider writing out your sales presentation and putting it on your website's home page. Or perhaps you could create a video of your sales presentation and include that on your website.

Making the Sale Online

There are several advantages to selling on-line, like the ability to make money while you sleep. However, there are challenges too. The biggest difficulty when selling over the internet is getting visitors to your website to trust you enough to make a purchase. It is vitally important that you display a professional appearance and build a virtual relationship with your potential customers.

Several common techniques to build trust on your website

include being approachable and friendly.

- **Create an About page to describe who you are**. Include a picture to show you are a real person. Having a name and a face makes buyers less fearful that you will take their money and not deliver a product.

- **Create a blog to share your knowledge and experience.** If you know a lot about your product, show your website visitors by writing a few blog posts. Start with at least three blog posts and try to add a new one at least once a week. Sharing information without charging for it is an excellent way to build trust and establish yourself as an expert.

- **Answer questions on a FAQ (Frequently Asked Questions) page.** One of the difficulties with internet sales is that your customers cannot easily or quickly ask you questions. You must anticipate their questions and compose your answers on a FAQ page. It is common to see website merchants answer questions like, "How can I make a return?" or "What if I am not satisfied?" Answer these common questions on a FAQ page and your customers will feel that you will take

Offer a chance to win a prize in exchange for an email address. I offer a kit at my convention booth. It has a copy of *Starting a Micro Business*, a sales receipt book, calculator, and office supplies in a basket. Visitors to my booth can win the start up kit by filling out a slip of paper with their name, cell phone number and email. At the end of the convention, I have dozens of names to add to my mailing list and I choose one to win the basket.

care of them.

- **Use an email list.** If a customer seems interested in your business, but not ready to place an order, ask if they would like to be on your mailing list. It is helpful to have a sign up sheet for them to list their names and addresses or e-mail addresses. If you have a website, you can create an electronic mailing list and ask people to give their name and email address.

Getting Paid Online

If your customers order on-line, you must have a secure payment system, such as Paypal or one of the numerous shopping cart programs. Use a stable and popular shopping cart program to collect credit card numbers. You, as the merchant, should not have access to your customers' credit card numbers.

Research shopping cart programs. Some are very user friendly and cost a bit more. Other shopping carts are free, but you must do a lot of setup or even software coding yourself. Visit several websites to see what shopping cart programs they use and then ask the owner for an opinion. Many programs offer a free trial period so you can test it out before you buy.

Make ordering easy and automatic for your customers. I ordered an ebook on video blogs, but I was not directed to a website to download the ebook. I thought perhaps the book was being emailed to me since the shopping cart had requested a mailing address. I emailed the website owner and waited a week until she returned from her vacation to receive my ebook! This is a poor way to do business online. It is easier on you and your customer to set up an automatic download by using a program such as **Click-bank.com.**

Follow up each purchase with a thank you email. Some programs will do this automatically. Share your email on your website so customers can contact you if they have a problem. Consider having a return policy posted clearly on your website.

Important Points

- A sales statement emphasizes the main benefits to the customer.

- Selling techniques can be very different depending on whether you meet your customers in person or sell on-line.

- A sales presentation is a bit like a live TV commercial, except you deliver it in person to potential customers.

- To move from a sales pitch to completing a sale, try asking questions and using forms.

- There are several techniques to use to get paid including making statements or using forms.

- If clients do not pay you, try some new techniques or create payment policies.

- The biggest difficulty when selling over the internet is getting visitors to trust you enough to make a purchase.

- If your customers order on-line, you must have a secure payment system.

Chapter Two
Marketing

You may have a great idea for a micro business. Your product or service is brilliant. It will help people, save them time, money, or frustration. You are bound to be a success and everyone you ask tells you so. But if you cannot find the people to buy your life-changing item, you will not succeed. Having a great product or service is not enough, you also have to find customers and meet a need that they have. That's where marketing comes in.

Describing your customer will help you come up with ideas on how to reach them. In this chapter, you will learn dozens of ways to reach your target market near and far and create a marketing plan.

Describe Your Customer

The golden rule for every business man is this:
Put yourself in your customer's place.
Orison Marden, founder of *Success* magazine

When you wrote your marketing plan in *Starting a Micro Business,* you had to answer some questions defining your customer and how you will reach them. Those might have been pretty tough questions to answer. Maybe you even left them blank because you did not know how to reach your potential customers. This chapter will give you a few ideas and tips.

Let's start by drawing a word picture of your typical customer.

>What is their age and gender?
>
>Where do they go? List physical places and on-line sites
>
>What do they read? List books, magazines, websites
>
>What websites do they visit?
>
>What do they do with their free time?
>
>What do they spend money on?

Here are some examples to guide you.

Sarah's Saddle Blankets
Describe a typical customer. *Horse owner*

What is their age and gender? *Teenage girls*

Where do they go? *They attend horse competitions and shows, boarding stables, parks, and farms.*

What do they read? *EQUUS magazine, Horse Illustrated, Horse & Rider*

What websites do they visit? *Horse.com, HorseCity.com, NewRider.com*

What do they do with their free time? *Ride their horses, attend horse shows*

What do they spend money on? *Their horse! Boarding fees and vet bills*

From thinking about her customer, Sarah decides to sell her handmade saddle blankets at horse competitions and shows. She cannot compete with the big websites that sell saddle blankets, but she does have a small website to show off her unique handmade blankets. She had some postcards printed with her website and color pictures of her blankets and left the postcards at a few boarding stables and with the local horse vet to pass out to his customers. Sarah also leaves samples of fabric at some of the stables. She is not taking orders over the internet, but interested customers can e-mail her and discuss placing an order.

Ryan's Tutoring Service

Describe a typical customer. *Struggling math students*

What is their age and gender? *12-17 year-olds*

Where do they go? *School, football games, soccer practice, music lessons*

What do they read? *Not much*

What websites do they visit? *Facebook*

What do they do with their free time? *Play video*

games, watch movies, play sports, sleep

What do they spend money on? *iTunes, food, clothes, cars*

Ryan defines his customers pretty well, but that didn't help him figure out how to reach them. Instead, his business mentor told him to concentrate on reaching the students' parents. When Ryan thought that way, his answers were different.

Describe a typical customer. *Parents of struggling math students*

What is their age and gender? *age 30-50+ year- olds*

Where do they go? *Work, their kids' sports games, concerts and plays where their kids perform*

What do they read? *Newspapers, information from the school, magazines on hobbies and parenting*

What websites do they visit? *News sites, parenting websites*

What do they do with their free time? *Drive their kids places*

What do they spend money on? *Their kids!*

Ryan came up with some great marketing ideas. He went to the math teachers in his school and asked to be recommended as a math tutor. He gave each teacher 20 fliers to send home with struggling students. They were on bright paper to be eye-catching. He also put fliers on cars at a football game. Finally, he asked his mom to post an electronic ad for his tutoring service on the parent forum of his school's website and on a local moms' social networking website that she visited.

If your initial answers fail to give you marketing ideas, go back and ask the questions from a different angle, like Ryan. Maybe you will find a new way to reach your customers.

Reaching Your Local Market

The customers for your micro business may be nearby in your hometown or far away and reached by the internet. Marketing to local customers is very different from reaching across the miles, so I have broken down these ideas into two groups. If your micro business has clients both near and far, you can gather ideas from both lists.

Reaching a Local Market

- Fliers or brochures. Display your fliers at libraries, community centers, gyms, art stores and bulletin boards. Put them on cars where your customers congregate such as sporting events, school events, and church services. It is polite to ask permission from the school or organization first. Replace the fliers every few months if they are removed.

- Postcards. These can be mailed to potential customers or handed out like fliers. Leave a few at local businesses like hair salons or stores where your potential customers might shop.

- Business cards. Like fliers and postcards, leave these everywhere a potential customer might see them. I have seen business cards displayed at grocery stores, car washes, and libraries.

- E-mails to local friends, networks and family. Email is cheap and fast. Ask your friends to spread the word and ask your parents to email their friends. People skim emails quickly, so your message should be short but have the important details like your tag line and what you charge. Add your contact information to the bottom of every e-mail you send. This can be set up automatically in your webmail server.

- Local social networks like city-based web forums. Use your parents' networks, too. I advertised for my daughter's tutoring business on my city-wide homeschool forum and a parent e-mail list. She picked up several students that way.

- Articles in local papers. E-mail a local reporter with a story about your business. They may do a feature on you and your micro business. Make sure they mention your name and contact information so potential customers know how to reach you.

- Press releases to local papers. Press releases are similar to articles, but you write them and submit them to the paper. Several helpful websites describe how to write a press release. One of my favorites is **www.publicityhound.com.**

- Word of mouth. Ask current customers to recommend you to their friends and neighbors. Offer a discount of 10-20% for every referral, if you wish. Give them a postcard or flier that they can hand to their friends.

- Trade shows, flea markets, craft shows. This might involve renting booth space, so consider the cost. You will have to have your sales presentation ready to go. Make your booth attract attention with live demonstrations, samples, bright posters, or even a candy dish. Have fliers, order forms, and business cards ready.

Reaching a Distant Market

Create a Website or Blog

It is essential to have a website or blog for your customers to learn more about you and your product or service. Take some time to learn how to create a website. Most large webhosts such as **1and1.com** have free website building tools offering simple, static websites. Try to avoid spending money on building a website as long as possible. Naturally, you must pay for the webhosting service, but you can find packages for as little as $5 a month.

Consider using a free blog platform such as Wordpress or Blogger to be your website. My site, **MicroBusinessFor-Teens.com** is built as a Wordpress blog. I needed a bit of help with it, so I did hire a blog expert, Kelly McCausey of **Freshnets.com.** I used **MomWebs.com** as the webhost. They have some very affordable start up packages, and you don't have to be a mom to use them (it's just a marketing angle).

To learn more, search on-line for "Wordpress tutorials," and you will find websites, books, and You Tube videos to get you started. Wordpress has a "New to Blogging" tutorial at **Wordpress.org.**

Alternatively, you can try a class offered by web-guru Kelly McCausey. She teaches a 15-week on-line course on blogging called Smart Blogging Skills. Visit **SmartBloggingSkills.com.**

Articles

Writing articles for others to read on the web can direct people to your website, especially if you are an expert or have unique knowledge. **Ezinearticles.com** is one of the best and biggest article websites. You can sign up for a free account, write informative articles on a topic of your choice and include your name and website at the end. It is an easy way to show yourself as knowledgeable in your area and help people find your website. Your article may even be republished in a newspaper, website, blog, or magazine.

Jonathan Hinton is a chess expert. The 19-year-old college freshman holds the title of National Master from the United States Chess Federation. He writes articles relating to his experiences at playing chess abroad and has co-authored a book, *Wojo's Weapons: Winning With White*, with International Master Dean Ippolito. I heard about Jonathan at a graduation party where I met his mother. She told me how Jonathan made money from chess. "Do you mean prize money?" I asked. "No," she explained, "by writing magazine articles and books."

E-mail Lists

Your email list is not your personal email list of friends and family, but rather a highly targeted list of people who have indicated an interest in your business or product. Many internet marketers will tell you that your mailing list is a gold mine. It is more valuable to your business than you may realize.

You can create a mailing list of interested people by asking visitors to your website to subscribe to your email list. Most web sites have a small box in the upper right corner where a visitor can enter their name and email address to be a part of your email list. You can then email your customers when you have a new product, a sale, or exciting news. Offer an enticement to get people to sign up for your mailing list by offering a free article, report, or mini ebook.

Your webhost may provide an email list service for free (**MomWebs.com** does!). It may have some limitations such as the number of names on your list, but you can't beat the price. There are also some primo email services like **Aweber.com** and **ConstantContact.com** that typically charge $20/month, so it may be something you consider in the future.

Newsletters or Ezines
After you have a mailing list, keep in touch with your customers by creating a newsletter or an ezine. They are very similar. An ezine is a bit longer than a newsletter, more like a short magazine with articles that you have written. A newsletter usually has only one article and then other information on products, sales, or general news.

Creating a newsletter can be a lot of fun if you like writing and communicating. You can use a program like Microsoft Publisher with its built in newsletter templates, or use a simpler program such as Microsoft Word or Open Office's free word processor, Write.

Internet Ads
You have probably been to a website that has a small section of Google ads put on the site by Google or the site owner. The advertiser pays for every time a person clicks on the ad. The pay-per-click fee can range from a few pennies to several dollars depending on the popularity of the website. Before you sign up for Google Ads or any on-line

advertising, do plenty of reading about it first. Start with free publicity and only pay for ads after your micro business can afford it.

On-line Surveys
People like giving their opinion, and putting a survey on your website or in an email can get people interested in your website, products, or services. You can ask customers questions about themselves, like "What websites do you visit?" or ask questions that help your business such as, "How much would you pay for an overnight babysitter?"

One of my favorite on-line survey tools is **Survey-Monkey.com.** You can have up to 10 questions with their free survey. Take my Micro Business survey at **www.surveymonkey.com/s/ZSH2LCT**.

Social Networking Sites
Facebook and other social networking sites are becoming more than a place to chat with friends. They are now marketing tools. On Facebook, businesses can have a Page (it used to be called a fan page) and post updates about their business. Friends and customers can "like" your page (it used to be called becoming your fan) and word about your business will spread. To learn about marketing on Facebook, I bought *Facebook Marketing for Dummies*. I also searched YouTube.com videos to learn more. My Facebook page is **www.Facebook.com/ MicroBusinesForTeens.com**.

Affiliate Programs
If you like a product or website, why not promote it on your site and make a commission? Many ebook authors will share up to 50% of their sale with you when the sale

comes through your website. The commission acts as a "Thank you" for sending a customer their way.

Internet Radio/Podcasts
Would you rather talk than write? Consider using internet radio or a podcast to market your micro business. You can record a show with only you talking, or you can have a guest that shares his or her knowledge.

One service I really like is **Talkshoe.com**. I have been both a guest and a host of Talkshoe shows. As a guest, I usually call in by telephone, and the host and I start talking. Then the host hits a record button to begin recording the show. You can then download the show to your website. It is simple and free!

Videos
You may best connect with your market via video. Creating a video can be a fun way to introduce your micro business. Post the video on YouTube or another video sharing site and your website. Video blogs (called vlogs) are short, two - or three-minute videos that you use instead of a written blog post. Encourage your email list and social network to watch your videos and word will spread!

Progress Step by Step

The only limit to your impact is your imagination and commitment.
Tony Robbins, self-help author

Try not to be overwhelmed by all these marketing methods. Start with just a few, such as business cards, fliers, and a simple website. Then, as you learn more about your customers, add new marketing tools such as testimonials or social networking. You do not have to do everything at once. Start small and build your business over time for lasting success.

Make a Marketing Plan

Since I advise you to progress one step at a time with marketing your micro business, it seems logical to have a plan.

1. Create a chart that lists all the various methods of reaching your market (posters, a website email, etc.). Then list the people you could reach with each marketing tool.

2. Set a goal such as the number of fliers to print or phone calls to make.

3. Map out specific steps to reach the goal such as designing a flier or practicing a sales pitch.

4. Create a specific plan for this week or this month.

5. Work the plan!

Example

Catherine wants to start a babysitting service. She lists some ways to find customers including fliers, phone calls and e-mails. To tell her friends she is willing to babysit if they are not available, she decides to start with email. Next she will send fliers to neighbors and make phone calls, but she puts off the idea of a website and business cards until a little later.

Here would be Catherine's work plan for this week. Next week she may have a different plan.

Today:
- Create an email or social network post: "I can babysit if you can't!" and sent it to 10 friends that I know do a lot of babysitting.

This week:
- Design a flier
- Make up a list of people I can call

Friday:
- Print out 25 copies of fliers
- Practice what to say on phone call

Saturday:
- Distribute fliers to neighbors
- Make four phone calls

Sunday:
- Give fliers to church friends
- Make four more phone calls

I do not think there is any other quality so essential to success of any kind as the quality of perseverance. It overcomes almost everything, even nature.
John D. Rockefeller

Marketing does not happen by itself. It is a continuous and never-ending task. Even super-successful companies, like

Apple, continue to invest time and money into marketing. Some people say marketing is the engine that will drive your business. Do not think of marketing as a one-time shot; plan to continue some marketing activity every month. In my example, Catherine plans to remind her friends every month that she is available to babysit. She will also hand out fliers to neighbors and church families every three months. These tactics refresh their memory about Catherine's babysitting service.

Important Points

- Describing your customer helps you to understand how to reach them.
- Use several methods to reach local customers.
- Different methods may be needed to reach distant customers.
- Create a marketing plan.
- Work the plan!
- Be persistent and keep marketing your business.

Chapter Three
Customer Service

Do what you do so well that they will want to see it again and bring their friends.
Walt Disney

Walt Disney obviously knew what he was talking about. Almost every American family wants to make a trip to Disney World at least once and many return year after year. It seems maintaining happy customers is the key to Disney's success. They keep customers happy and coming back. Disney is a role model for customer service.

Serving Customers Is Good for Business

Customer service is important because you need customers to continue to hire you and you want your customers to tell others about your business. Word-of-mouth is the best kind of advertising because it is very effective and costs nothing. However, word-of-mouth advertising can work against you too. If you do not treat your customers well, they will not come back. They may give their friends negative comments about you and you will be out of business very quickly.

> ***If you make customers unhappy in the physical world, they might each tell 6 friends. If you make customers unhappy on the Internet, they can each tell 6,000 friends.***
> Jeff Bezos, Founder of Amazon.com

When my children were young, I was looking for a babysitter and asked my neighbor about a girl who lived down the street. "I wouldn't hire Megan," she told me. "She usually forgets if you don't remind her at least twice. I've had her not show up several times." That told me all I wanted to know. I found another babysitter. When you are late for a job, you disappoint the customer and hurt your reputation and future business.

Customer service is important for more than business success. You should respect your customers because they are human beings. That's it—just because they are people and should be treated with dignity.

A teenage bagger at my local grocery store was complaining about two customers that did not speak English. "Why don't they learn English or go back where they came from?" I heard him say. I hope he never goes into business for himself because he did not understand customer service, nor could he treat a stranger (perhaps a foreign visitor to his country) with basic human dignity. Customer service means that we treat people with respect simply because they are people.

What to Charge

The absolute fundamental aim is to make money out of satisfying customers.
Sir John Egan, CEO of Jaguar

A large component of customer service is charging a fair price. Many micro business owners struggle with what a fair price is for their services or products. If they charge too much, they may not attract customers. However if they charge too little, they may not cover their costs or make a decent profit.

Here are some tips for setting a price on which you and your customers agree.

- **Do a market survey.** Ask potential clients what they are willing to pay. You may be surprised at what some people will offer for your unique service or product.

- **Learn what your competitors charge.** You can ask a competitor directly or ask customers what they have paid in the past. A teenager giving piano lessons asked several other teenagers and parents what the going rate for beginning piano lessons was to help her set her price.

- **Cover your costs.** You must know what your costs are and then add to it your desired profit. One unfortunate micro business owner charged only enough to cover her costs, forgetting to make a profit or pay herself.

45

- **Remember taxes.** Work with an accountant to calculate what you will owe in federal, state, and local income taxes. As a micro business owner, you will also pay self-employment tax (Social Security and Medicare). Accountants frequently advise small business owners to set aside 25-35% of their profit to pay for taxes. You may need to increase your price, just to pay the taxes to the government. Learn more about paying taxes in my book, *Money and Taxes in a Micro Business.*

- **Value your time.** Some micro owners charge by the hour they spend with a customer (such as tutoring by the hour), but forget that they spend many hours outside of the meeting. Travel time and preparation time should be considered when you set an hourly rate.

- **Adjust your price when needed.** Adjust your prices if your costs increase or if you find you are seriously under priced compared to your competitors. Also increase your prices if you find a high demand for your product or service.

- **Adjust your prices as you gain experience.** Customers value an experienced worker more than a new one. After a few years of running her micro business, one owner made a plan to increase her rates and began charging new clients a higher rate and increased her rates to current clients over a two year period.

Tips and Secrets of Customer Service

Too many people think only of their own profit. But business opportunity seldom knocks on the door of self-centered people. No customer ever goes to a store merely to please the storekeeper.
Kazuo Inamori, creator of the Kyoto Prize

Although the concept seems simple, hundreds of books written about customer service offer tips and "secrets" to serving customers. The heart of customer service is to give your customers what they paid for while treating them with respect. That is pretty simple, but there are numerous ways to show respect and to serve a customer. Here are some tips for relating to your customers.

- Smile! A smile can really make you seem friendly, warm, and caring. Friendly people attract others.

- Shake hands. Offer your hand when first meeting a potential customer. This might make you feel uncomfortable because teenagers do not usually shake hands when meeting a new person. However, adults in the business world frequently offer their

I was giving a workshop on micro businesses for teenagers at a convention when a 12-year-old boy came up to me after the program, extended his hand and said, "Hello, I'm Jack. I really liked your presentation." I was immediately impressed by Jack because he offered his hand to me. Although he was young and small in stature, I knew in an instant that this young man would be good at whatever he set his mind to.

hand when being introduced. Practice on friends or your family if you need to get comfortable shaking hands.

- Look them in the eye. Making eye contact shows confidence if you feel timid or nervous. Looking directly at someone is also a sign of respect.

My husband was being introduced to a four-year-old boy, Allen, by his mother. Like most children, Allen hid his face rather than look at my husband. "Oh, no you don't!" Allen's mother told him. "You look Mr. Topp in the eye. If you don't want to say anything, you can just wave." We were amazed, but Allen lifted his head, looked at my husband, and gave a small wave. If a child can do it, you can too! I recommend offering your hand instead of waving, even though a four-year-old can get away with a wave. We were also impressed that Allen's mother was teaching him at a very young age how to meet and greet adults.

- Say "Please" and "Thank you." You cannot use these words too much. Your customers will respect your polite gestures if you say, "Mrs. Jones, may I please watch TV after the children are in bed?" or "Thank you so much for hiring me."

- Be on time. Call if you will be more than 5 minutes late. Such a gesture shows that you respect the customer's time. They more often forgive if you call ahead of time rather than make excuses when you arrive late.

- Leave the place cleaner than you found it. I hired a babysitter who washed the dishes I had left in the sink. I certainly did not expect her to do that, but she believed in leaving the kitchen cleaner than she found it. She went to the top of my babysitter list!

Here is a simple but powerful rule-always give people more than what they expect to get.
Nelson Boswell, author

- Give them more than they expected. One of my babysitters would bring a craft project along when she watched my daughters. At the end of the night, the kids not only had a good time, but had something to show for it too. This babysitter did more than was expected and my kids (and I) loved it!

- Consider giving something for free. A teenager had a dog sitting and dog walking micro business. He started making dog biscuits and feeding them to the dogs. He even left a few biscuits behind as a free sample for his customers. Customers soon started asking to buy the dog biscuits and telling their friends. The biscuit business became so successful that it surpassed the dog walking business and a new micro business was born.

- Apologize and give a refund. One of my tax clients called me to say that I had made an error on part of her tax return. I hate calls like that, but she was correct. I had made a mistake. I apologized for the error and told her I would refund some of my fee. I thought she might not return to me as a tax client the following year, but she did, probably because I had offered an apology and a refund.

No man fails who does his best.
Orison Marden, founder of *Success* magazine

- Be flexible. Change your schedule to accommodate customers as much as possible. Brady could not serve his lawn mowing customers when planned, so he offered them another time.

- Leave something they can pass along. When you finish a job, leave behind a business card or a flier printed on brightly colored paper. Consider buying magnetic business cards so your customers can stick them to their refrigerators. If you leave behind a card or flier, they have an opportunity to pass it along to a friend or neighbor.

> A woman at my church makes scented soaps. She carries very small sample soaps with a business card wrapped around them. I was happy to take home her sample when she passed them out at a church meeting.

- Dress nicely. Have clean, tear-free clothes. Remember to be extra aware of your clothing. Go for clean, modest clothes and T-shirts without messages. Overdressing for work is better than under dressing.

Clothes and manners do not make the man;
but, when he is made,
they greatly improve his appearance.
Henry Ward Beecher, clergyman and abolitionist

- Be friendly, but keep a level of professionalism with your clients. You can be friendly by asking general questions about their family such as ,"How was your vacation?" or "Any plans for the holiday?" However, don't invade their privacy with questions about their family relations or health.

- Give customers several ways to contact you. Make it easy for a customer to reach you by printing up business cards with your phone number and email address, or creating a website with an easy-to-remember name. Consider reserving your own name for a website. Tell your customers about your website and that it is the same as your name.

- Remember your customer's name and use it. Call adults Mr., Ms., or Mrs. unless invited to use their first name. Using those formal titles may feel uncomfortable to you, but they show respect.

- Listen to complaints and do not make excuses. When a customer complains, offer a listening ear. Consider a complaint as an opportunity to improve your business. Do *not* make an excuse. Excuses do not help and will only frustrate the customer. You may come across as a whiner who shirks responsibility.

> I hired my neighbor girl, Ruth, as an after-school babysitter. She called me Mrs. Topp, because her parents had taught her to show respect. Ruth is now a grown woman with children of her own. She still calls me Mrs. Topp, and it is a friendly term that we are both comfortable with using.

> ***Your most unhappy customers are your greatest source of learning.***
>
> Bill Gates in *Business @ the Speed of Thought*

- Make doing business easy for your customer. Consider going to their house to wash a car, walk a dog, or tutor a child. You can charge more to cover your transportation expenses and they might appreciate it enough to pay the difference.

- Never, ever argue. Arguing with customers never benefits anyone. Even if you know you are correct and they are wrong, don't fight. Simply say, "I'm sorry you see it that way. Thank you for your business." Take out your frustration somewhere else, like on a stuffed animal or a basketball court. Vent to your family about the situation, but never argue with a customer.

> My family waited for 45 minutes to be served at a restaurant. Meanwhile another family that had arrived after us was served first, and we couldn't find our waiter anywhere. We were getting frustrated and complained to the manager. When the waiter showed up, he started making excuses, "The cooks are slow; everything is backed up, etc." We would have appreciated an apology more than an excuse.

Remember not only to say the right thing in the right place, but far more difficult still, to leave unsaid the wrong thing at the tempting moment.

Benjamin Franklin

- Return phone calls and e-mails promptly. Customers like to hear back quickly. If you delay too long, they might hire someone else.

Take care of your customers, or someone else will.
Unknown

- Pleasantly surprise them. Be creative in how you surprise your customers. Hand write a thank you note, leave a sample, or offer a free service.

- Admit your mistakes. It takes a mature person to admit when they are wrong. Simply say, "I'm sorry. I made a mistake." You do not have to offer a reason or an excuse (excuses typically back-fire), just admit you were wrong and assure your customer that it will not happen again.

- Do not make them wait. If you find customers lining up to buy your products, acknowledge their presence and say, "I'll be right with you." If they do have to wait, apolo-

Doctors are notorious for running behind schedule. Imagine my surprise when my doctor entered the room and apologized for being 15 minutes late. "Sorry to keep you waiting," she said. "I was reviewing your chart." She apologized and I felt respected.

gize before you serve them. Apologizing can deflect a lot of impatience.

- Acknowledge them. Do not pretend you don't see a customer. I have stood at a counter while a clerk talked on the phone or waited on someone else, acting as though I did not exist. "Am I invisible?" I wondered. Instead, I feel valued when a busy clerk at least acknowledges my existence. Usually she says, "I'll be right with you," as she rushes past, but at least I know she saw me!

- Do a little extra. Go beyond what is expected. If you are hired to babysit a child, bring along a book or game he or she might like to borrow for a week. If you are hired to mow the grass, sweep the clippings off the sidewalk too. If someone buys a necklace, throw in an inexpensive bracelet.

One of the deep secrets of life is that all that is really worth doing is what we do for others.
Lewis Carroll, author of *Alice in Wonderland*

- Give options. Offer an upgrade on a service for an additional fee. If you do lawn care, offer to edge the walkways as an upgrade option. You can provide basic, deluxe, and grand packages of your services.

- Ask, "What else can I do for you?" If they answer, you will gain ideas of how to improve your services. Be sure to explain that you will add a small fee to their bill and ask, "Would that be okay with you?" They will probably agree.

- Ask, "Do you have any friends or neighbors

who could use me/my product?" This promotes word-of-mouth advertising. Be sure to have a few extra business cards or fliers they can pass on to friends.

I hope you can use some of these ideas in your micro business. It might be a good idea to review this list once or twice a year to get fresh ideas on customer service.

Important Points

- Customer service brings repeat customers.
- Happy customers will spread the word about you to their friends.
- Serve your customers simply because they are people and deserve respect.
- Set a fair price.
- Review customer service tips once or twice a year to get new ideas.

Chapter Four
Record Keeping

You may have heard that two-thirds of small businesses fail in their first three years. These statistics might explain why:

Frequency of Record Keeping	Survival Rate
At least monthly	79.7%
Quarterly	71.5%
Half yearly	49.9%
Annually	36.0%

Businesses that kept records at least monthly had a nearly 80% survival rate, yet business that updated their records only annually had a 36% survival rate.

Record keeping in business is like taking a pulse; your records, or "books," tell if your business is healthy. Many businesses fail because the owners do not check the health of their business often enough. Good record keeping is key to running a successful micro business.

What Records to Keep

There are several important records to keep when running your micro business:

1. A checking account or Paypal account to deposit income and pay expenses.

2. Documents such as checking account statements, credit card statements, invoices (bills from people to whom you owe money), and sales receipts (a copy of what you sold to customers).

3. Official government paperwork including tax returns, vendor licenses, your Employer Identification Number (EIN) from the Internal Revenue Service (IRS), and Doing Business As (DBA) name registration from your state.

4. Records of start up expenses you paid before you started your business such as website design, advertising, consulting with a CPA, etc.

5. Receipts for large purchases such as equipment or computers used in your micro business.

Record Transactions

For most micro businesses, the business checkbook is the main source for records. Most accountants recommend keeping a separate checking account for business and using it only for business expenses, not personal spending. However, this may be unnecessary for a teenage micro business because many teenagers do not have a personal checking account, much less a business account. I recommend that you open at least one checking account when you launch a micro business. It is not crucial to have two separate accounts, but it is important to keep good records.

If you use only one checking account for business and personal use, mark each transaction as business or personal. You could use a letter like "B" for business or "S" for self (or "P" for Personal) in the checkbook ledger.

Phil started a micro business and opened a business checking account. He did not have a personal checking account. When I was recording his transactions into QuickBooks, I noticed checks written to his high school for sports fees and a yearbook. These were clearly personal expenses and I marked them as such (called an "owner's draw") when I did his bookkeeping.

If you keep a separate business checking account and want to use some of the money for personal use, write a check to yourself or transfer some money out of your business checking account and into your personal checking account. Then spend the money.

This transfer is called an owner's draw, meaning that you, the owner, are drawing cash out of your business. An owner's draw is a perfectly legal and legitimate thing to do. These withdrawals are not business expenses and cannot be tax deductions, so they need to be clearly marked as owner's draws for personal expenses.

Keep all your checkbook statements, canceled checks, and deposit slips. I recommend buying duplicate checks because they provide a written record of your expenses. Many banks no longer return canceled checks and many are not keeping electronic backups for more than a year, so you must keep your own records of checkbook transactions.

A Bookkeeping System
On a regular basis (monthly at least) you should transfer your records from your checking account to your bookkeeping system, whether it is on paper or a computer spreadsheet. I cover the details of bookkeeping in Chapter Five. It may seem tedious and repetitive to copy all your transactions into a bookkeeping system, but doing so is vitally important to your business success.

If you have a very active micro business, you may wish to start using small business accounting software like Quick-Books. The beauty of QuickBooks is that you record the transaction only once and the software records it simultaneously into the checkbook and into your bookkeeping system. This way, financial statements can be created instantly. See Chapter Six, "Using Software" for more details.

Keep All Supporting Documents

Keep supporting documents such as bank statements,

sales slips, paid bills, invoices, receipts, and credit card sales slips. These documents contain information that you will need to record in your books and to prepare your tax return. It is helpful to organize them by category according to the type of income or expense. Some business owners store receipts by month, but it is better to organize them by category. Categorizing simplifies both locating documents and tax preparation.

Melissa scribbles the expense category on her receipts while it is fresh in her mind. This makes it easier to record each transaction in the correct category in her bookkeeping system and to file the receipt after she has recorded it.

File Folders

I find that an expanding file folder is an excellent, yet simple, storage system for supporting documents. Each folder can be used for each category of expense such as gas, office supplies, etc.

File receipts into folders after you have recorded them in your bookkeeping system, whether on paper or on your computer (more about that in the chapter on bookkeeping). Organize bank statements, official forms, and letters into file folders as well. Any remaining folders can store documents such as sales receipts and deposit slips.

Consider these names for your filing system:

- Income: sales receipts
- Checking: bank statements and deposit slips
- Paypal records

- Expenses: receipts. If your micro business is simple, all your expenses can go into one folder. As your business becomes more complex, I recommend using separate folders for major categories of expense. If you purchase goods or services on-line, print out the receipt and file it under Expenses also.
- Accounts Receivable: Keep a list of people that owe you money. Check off their names when they pay you.
- Accounts Payable: Keep a list of people to whom you owe money, such as your parents for a loan, or a friend who helped you in the business. Pull out the paper every month so you remember to pay these people.

Paypal Records

If you use Paypal or another electronic shopping cart system to make sales from your website, be sure to have a separate folder for Paypal monthly summaries of your income. Paypal will not mail these statements to you, so I suggest you print them out yourself.

Even in this digital age, you will need paper printouts to prove income and expenses for two reasons: the Internal Revenue Service (IRS) may want to see proof of your expenses on paper, and Paypal may not keep records longer than twelve months.

File by Category:

One major reason to keep good records is to lessen the amount of taxes you will pay. You are allowed to deduct (subtract) from your income all expenses related to your business. If you lose receipts or forget to record your expenses, you will have a mistakenly larger profit and, therefore, pay more tax on that profit.

Most business owners find that good record keeping saves them from over-paying on their taxes. The desire to lower their taxes is a strong motivator to establish a good filing system.

To make tax preparation simpler, file your paperwork according to categories that correspond to the sole proprietorship business tax return, Schedule C Business Income or Loss. This list is used for every business, small or large, so many of these categories may not apply to your business.

- Advertising. This should include your website fees. You may not have paperwork if you pay on-line, so keep your bank statement as proof of payment.

- Transportation. Keep a log of your business miles. The IRS requires a written record. Estimates of mileage are not enough. I keep a calendar with my business miles recorded on the proper date.

- Equipment and software purchases.

- Professional fees to accountants and lawyers. File the bill you receive from your accountant or lawyer after you pay it.

- Contract labor to hired professionals such as editors, web designers, etc.

- Office supplies.

- Purchases of items for resale (i.e., inventory). Keep receipts of anything you buy that you will resell. If you buy inventory on-line, print a copy of the receipt.

- Shipping supplies.

- Utilities, including your cell phone and internet bills. These should be separated into business and personal use. Use any reasonable method like the percentage of computer time you spend on your business versus personal time. Only the business portion is a tax deductible business expense.

Tell your accountant the total internet fees for the family and your business use percentage. He or she will do the math and put the correct number on the tax return.

- Wages paid to employees and payroll taxes.

- Other expenses including bank, merchant, and Paypal fees as well as professional development expenses for books and magazines you read or conferences you attend.

Some small businesses also keep categories called Miscellaneous for the little items that don't seem to fit anywhere. It is also a good practice to have a folder called "Ask My Accountant." These are expenses that you are unsure about deducting or need help in classifying.

Paper in an Electronic Age
After reading the following section, you may feel as if you will drown in papers, especially with paper copies of online payments, keeping Paypal records on paper, and so forth. In this electronic age, it might seem a bit ridiculous, but there are some legitimate reasons for keeping all this paper.

- You are running a micro business—probably your first business—so you should get used to record keeping on paper before you jump ahead into electronic records. It is a bit like learning to do long division on paper before being allowed to use a calculator.
- Paper provides a physical, tangible way to learn

bookkeeping. In college-level accounting classes, the students start with paper record keeping and only move onto using spreadsheets and software after learning the basic concepts.

- Paper is less expensive than accounting software.
- The IRS still expects to see paper receipts and proof of income on paper.

For now, as a micro business owner, it is best to keep paper records. As you gain experience in bookkeeping and running a business, you can move on to a paperless office. You can use software such as a spreadsheet or QuickBooks to help keep records, but you must still retain original documents, so keep those receipts!

Keep Official Letters From the IRS and State Governments

Keep copies of everything you mail to the Internal Revenue Service (IRS) and to state and city governments. Make a copy of checks you write to pay taxes (or use duplicate checks). Save every letter sent to or received from any government agency, especially confirmation of your EIN (Employer Identification Number), vendor licenses, and name registration.

Keep copies of your tax returns in folders marked by year. After the tax return has been filed, you can store the return and its corresponding support documents (such as expense receipts and sales receipts) in a large envelope or folder marked with the year.

Set up a file drawer or a file box to keep these important

records. Label your folders and stay organized with the paperwork.

Linda stayed very organized and sorted her paper-work into folders and her receipts by categories. At tax time, she pulled out her receipts, bundled them with a paper clip and a post-it note to give to me as I prepared her tax return. She also used Quick-Books to record her business transactions and in-ventory, so she had electronic as well as physical records. Her system was easy for her to manage and made it easy for me to prepare her tax return correctly.

Record keeping is the lifeblood of your business.

How to Record Your Start Up Expenses

In general, micro businesses have few start up expenses because the owner uses what he already has on hand. I encourage you to launch your business with as few start up expenses as possible. However, many times a micro business will have to spend a little money before the business starts on advertising, equipment, professional advice, etc. You should keep records of these expenses because they may be a tax deduction. Remember, good record keeping reduces the amount of taxes you pay on your profit.

You cannot deduct start up expenses before a business begins, only after you have started the business.

Cindy wanted to start a business making and selling

crafts. She spent $250 buying supplies and paid an accountant for advice, but she never sold any of her crafts. She cannot deduct the $250 this year. She must keep a record of these expenses and consider them start up expenses for when she really does start her business.

Start up expenses can include anything that you might legitimately deduct as a business expense, such as:
- website design fees
- vendor license or name registration fees
- mileage
- advertising
- education related to your business (like the price of this book)
- professional advice from an accountant or lawyer

Start a list or a spreadsheet like this:

	Date	Amount
Website design		
Advertising		
Mileage		
Professional fees		
Equipment		
Supplies		
Licenses or government fees		
Other		

Notice that on the list of start up expenses I did not include buying inventory. You will need initial inventory if you are going to sell something, but inventory is not a start up expense. The cost of your inventory is deducted as you sell it, as a term called *cost of goods sold*.

When Does a Business Start?

Sometimes it is difficult to know when your business actually starts. If a small business has a storefront or a shop, it is easy to know when it begins—the day it opens for business. However, some micro businesses start as a hobby or as volunteer work before becoming a business, so it is a bit harder to tell when the business starts. Here are some guidelines to follow:

Sarah volunteered to design a website for Sue's Salon. Sarah did it for the experience and fun and was surprised when Sue handed her a check for $70. All of a sudden, Sarah was in business! Her micro business started the day that Sue paid her for the website.

- You are paid by your first customer
- You launch a website
- You advertise your business
- You accept your first customer or project, start work, and expect to be paid later.

Typically, start up expenses cannot be deducted in the first year of a business. They must be spread out over 60 months (called *amortization*). However, in 2010, the Internal Revenue Service (IRS) lets small businesses deduct $10,000 in start up expenses in their first year of operation. Any extra start up expenses are spread out (amortized) over the next 180 months (15 years).

IRS Publication 535 Business Expenses has more details

on what qualifies as a start up expense **(http://www.irs.gov/publications/p535/)**

The important point to remember is to keep records on your start up expenses and discuss them with your accountant. He or she will help fill in the tax forms to deduct most, if not all, of your start up expenses correctly.

Claire wanted to turn her painting hobby into a micro business. She owned a lot of equipment that she had bought over several years, including an easel, canvases, paint, and brushes. All of these expenses could be considered start up expenses, but she purchased them so long ago that she no longer had the receipts or knew what they had cost. She will probably not be able to deduct these as start up expenses on her tax return.

Record Purchases of Equipment

If you buy equipment that will last more than one year, it is treated differently for tax purposes than your day-to-day expenses. These long-lived items are called *capital expenses.* Think of capital as being large or major. A capital expense must usually be spread out and deducted on your tax return over several years. This process is called *depreciation.* The method for depreciating an item depends on its "useful life" as defined by the IRS based on the type of equipment.

Examples of Capital Expenses
Capital expenses in a micro business may include any of

the following:
- Furniture
- Tools, including drills, power saws, etc.
- Automobiles
- Machinery, such as lawn mowers
- Computers, including printers and software
- Equipment such as microwaves, cameras, guitars, etc.

Office supplies are not considered long-lived assets because businesses typically use up office supplies in a year. Likewise, low-cost items are not considered capital expenses because their dollar value is small.

The IRS does not specifically define "low cost items." A rough rule of thumb for a teenage micro business owner is to consider anything over $250 as a capital expense. Your accountant can help you decide on whether an item is a capital expense (and, therefore, depreciated over time) or a typical day-to-day expense.

Some of these concepts are complicated. Rather than explain the minute details of accounting to you, I will focus on what records you need to keep and share with your accountant. He or she can then advise you and prepare your tax return correctly.

Why Capital Expenses Are Treated Differently
Capital expenses are treated differently on your tax return from other purchases. When you buy $100 in office supplies, you can deduct $100 on your tax return and pay lower taxes. But capital expenses are long-lived, so you deduct the expense over the life of the property. Theoretically, these large cost, long-lived items will help you make

more income in your business for a long time. They are really business assets. Assets are anything a business owns that help to make money such as equipment, inventory, and cash in the bank.

Your accountant can help you prepare your tax return correctly. Accountants know all the IRS rules on the expected life of business equipment. For now, you just need to know what capital expenses are and be familiar with what records to keep.

What Records to Keep for Capital Expenses

Keep records on your purchases of any capital (major, long lived) expenses and give them to your accountant.

- The item, property, or equipment purchased, such as computers, cameras, lawn mowers, etc.
- Purchase date
- Cost, including shipping and sales tax
- Percent used for business. This can be determined by the hours used for business or personal use.

For example, Charlie purchased a new computer and uses it 75% of the time for school and personal use and 25% for business. He also purchased software and uses it only for doing graphic design for his micro business, so business use is 100%. Charlie's records would look like this:

Property	Date	Amount	Percent Business Use
Computer	March 30	$850.00	25.00%
Graphic Design Software	March 30	$450.00	100.00%

I hope this chapter has reinforced the need to keep good records, primarily to lower your tax bill, but also for you to understand where your money is coming and going. In the following chapter on bookkeeping I will help you record all this information you have kept in a way that will be helpful to you in running your micro business.

Important Points

- Keep records in a checkbook.
- Separate business and personal expenses.
- Keep supporting documents and receipts in a file folder.
- Organize receipts by categories.
- Plan carefully for start up expenses.
- Record the right information when buying property or equipment.

Chapter Five
Bookkeeping Basics

Keeping good records is vital to the success of a business. What should you, as a micro business owner, do to make sure your record keeping is done correctly? You could learn bookkeeping or take an accounting class, but, as a teenager, you may already have a full academic load. You could hire a bookkeeper, but that can become expensive. I have found that there are simpler ways to keep good records and this chapter will teach you those methods.

A Simple Bookkeeping Method

You do not have to study accounting or hire a bookkeeper to start a micro business. It might be a good idea to take a bookkeeping or accounting class after running your business for a year or so, but right now all you need is a little training in how to keep your business records.

I have several micro business clients that use my accounting services only for tax preparation. They do all their own record keeping. I offer them advice on recording transactions. Sometimes I even train a micro business owner to use QuickBooks. A few clients grow to a point that they hire a bookkeeper to do their bookkeeping. These are usually adults who work full-time in their business. Hiring help allows them to concentrate on running their business.

For now, I will show you a simple method of bookkeeping that involves single-entry bookkeeping, not double-entry bookkeeping that is taught to accountants. Just get some paper or a computer spreadsheet and follow these three easy steps.

Step 1: List all your sources of income
Typical sources of income in a micro business include:
- Sales of services such as music lessons, babysitting, lawn mowing, etc. If you offer several services, list each separately.
- Sale of products such as T-shirts, craft items, jewelry, etc.
- Interest earned from a savings account. Usually teenagers save money in their personal savings account, but perhaps you have plans to expand your business and are saving money for the business, not your personal use. If so, list the income earned on that savings as business income.
- Sale of assets. This is when you sell equipment that you used in your business such as a computer or a lawn mower. This happens rarely, maybe once every couple of years. Selling products from your inventory

on a regular basis is not the sale of assets, but is recorded under sale of products.

Example: Charlie has a graphic design micro business, creating button ads for websites. His buttons are his products and he lists them under Product Sales. Charlie just upgraded his computer and is selling his old computer. The money from the sale of his old computer is a Sale of Assets. Although this distinction seems overly picky, it is an important concept in business.

Charlie lists his Income Categories as these:

Income from Charlie's Graphic Design Micro Business
>   Product Sales (graphic buttons and banners)
>   Sale of Assets (old computer)

Some micro business owners use a simple spreadsheet called an Income Ledger to record their income. As an example, Charlie would list his two sources of income as this:

Income Ledger

Date	Source	Amount
1/10/20xx	Product: Client A ad design	$250.00
1/25/20xx	Sale of Assets: Sold old computer	$75.00

Step 2: List all your expenses
You should create another spreadsheet (called ledgers in bookkeeping lingo) for your expenses. The simplest method is to list all your expenses on one sheet.

Charlie, the website ad button designer, has only a few business expenses, so he lists them all on one sheet.

Expenses Ledger

Date	Source	Amount
1/09/20xx	Website fee	$20.00
1/11/20xx	Ink at office store	$12.00
1/11/20xx	New computer	$427.38
1/15/20xx	Brochures	$32.00
1/15/20xx	Lunch with client	$8.50
1/30/20xx	Stamps	$ 55.00

Another method to record expenses is to use categories. I recommend you use categories listed on the IRS tax form for small businesses called Schedule C Profit or Loss from Business. Take a look at it here: **http://www.irs.gov/pub/ irs-pdf/f1040sc.pdf.**

The following table lists the expenses listed on the Schedule C. Check which ones you will use in your business, but they may not all apply. On the other hand, this list does not include everything you might spend in your business. For example, website fees are not listed. I would classify them as an advertising expense. This list was created by the IRS many years ago and has not been changed in decades. Add any of your expenses that are not listed (like Paypal fees) at the bottom.

Expense Category	I'll use it
Advertising (including website fees)	
Auto (mileage)	
Contract Labor	
Depreciation	
Insurance	
Legal and Professional fees	
Office Supplies	
Rent (equipment or space or a building)	
Supplies (other than office supplies)	
Sales tax and licenses	
Travel & meals	
Utilities (cell phone and internet)	
Wages to employees	
Other:	

To continue our example, Charlie picks the categories of expense he will use frequently. He adds a column to his records and it looks like this:

Expenses Ledger

Date	Source	Category	Amount
1/09/200X	Website fee	Advertising	$20.00
1/11/200X	Ink at office store	Office Supplies	$12.00
1/11/200X	New computer	Equipment	$427.38
1/15/200X	Brochures	Advertising	$32.00
1/15/200X	Lunch with Client B	Meals	$8.50
1/30/200X	Stamps	Office Supplies	$ 55.00

If you are not sure how to classify an expense, you can ask your accountant.

If your micro business buys and sells products, you will also need to keep good records of your inventory called Cost of Goods Sold (or COGS). COGS includes buying items to re-sell as well as shipping and packaging expenses. Check which, if any, of the COGS categories you might use in your micro business.

Cost of Goods Sold Categories	I'll use it
Product Purchase	
Shipping Expense	
Packaging (boxes, tape, etc.)	
Other Cost of Goods Sold	

Example: Rusty runs a dog walking and pet sitting business. He has also expanded his micro business to add in doggie treats that his customers love (or rather their *dogs* love the biscuits).

Rusty has some typical expenses for a dog walking business and because he sells doggie biscuits, he must also track his Cost of Goods Sold (COGS) expenses. Rusty purchases inventory and packages them for his customers, but he hand delivers the doggie biscuits, so there is no shipping expense.

Rusty's Dog Walking and Biscuit Business
Income
     Dog Walking Service
     Pet Sitting Service

Sale of Doggie Biscuits

Expenses
Advertising (his website and fliers)
Office Expense (paper and ink for his printer)
Professional and Legal fees (an hour with an accountant for advice)
Sales Tax
Supplies (extra leash to use for walking dogs)

Cost of Goods Sold
Purchases of inventory (purchase of doggie biscuits)
Packaging

Step 3: Create Record Keeping Forms

You can keep your business records on paper as Charlie did in our example. I recommend accounting ledgers with columns that you can buy at an office supply store or use a spreadsheet.

Here is a variation that many micro business owners use. Instead of one column for all your expenses, make several columns, one for each of your expense categories. This may mean you turn the page sideways or buy some ledger paper. If you are using the computer, adding columns to a spreadsheet is very easy!

Charlie could expand his columns for his graphic design business to display several areas of expenses as shown on the next page.

Want a free spreadsheet program? Download the open source program called CALC from Open Office. It looks and works just like Microsoft Excel.
www.openoffice. org/product/ calc.html

Month of: January

Date	Check Number	Description	Income	Advertising	Office Supplies	Meals	Mileage	Equipment (Capital Expense)
1/09/20xx	Debit card	Website fee		$20.00				
1/10/20xx		Income from Client A	$250.00					
1/11/20xx	Debit card	New computer						$427.38
1/11/20xx	203	Ink at office store			$12.00			
1/15/20xx	204	Brochures		$32.00				
1/15/20xx	cash	Lunch with Client B				$8.50		
		Mileage to lunch meeting					12	
01/25/20xx		Sold old computer	$75.00					
1/30/20xx	Debit card	Stamps			$55.00			
1/30/20xx		Mileage to post office					6	
Totals			$325.00	$52.00	$67.00	$8.50	$18.00	$427.38

The advantage to this variation is that you will see totals by category. You can easily see where your money is going. Your accountant will also appreciate this at tax time.

What to Do and When

All too often, I find that micro business owners enjoy running their businesses and making money, but put off the tedious task of bookkeeping. Unfortunately, this can become a bad habit. If you only record your expenses at the end of the year, your micro business is likely to fail. Remember the chart at the beginning of Chapter Four on Record Keeping? It showed that if a business owner does bookkeeping on a monthly basis, there is an 80% chance of success.

What to Do Daily
When I recommend you do some bookkeeping tasks daily, I do not mean every day. Just do these tasks on the same day you receive income or pay an expense. I can best explain the daily tasks by an example of Rusty's Dog Walking Business.

> Rusty's dog walking business is going well. On Tuesday, June 8, he walked Mrs. Jones' dog and earned $8.00 paid in cash. Rusty puts the cash into an envelope labeled Dog Walking Income. After he gets home, he records $8.00 on the date he earned it. He also checked in on Snoopy, the Johnson's dog while they are on vacation. He will get paid for pet sitting Snoopy when the Johnsons return on Saturday.
>
> On Saturday, June 12, Rusty walks Mrs. Jones' dog again and receives another $8.00 in cash. The John-

sons come home from vacation and they pay him $25 by check for dog sitting. Rusty puts the check in another envelope labeled Pet Sitting Income.

On Saturday, Rusty deposits $41.00 from his dog walking and pet sitting services. Rusty goes to Office Depot to pick up some fliers he had printed to advertise his business and buy more paper and ink. Rusty marks his receipt from Office Depot as "Advertising" next to the cost of the fliers and "Office" next to the paper and ink costs. Rusty likes to separate his expenses into different categories, so he can track how much he is spending on advertising. (He is a perfect example of doing proper bookkeeping!).

When Rusty, gets home he records his income and expenses in his spreadsheet. It looks like this:

	A	B	C	D	E	F
1	Rusty's Dog Walking and Biscuit Business					
2						
3	Date	Check Number	Description	Income	Advertising	Office Supplies
4	06/08/10		Walked Jones dog	$8.00		
5	06/12/10		Johnson Pet Sitting	$25.00		
6	06/12/10		Walked Jones dog	$8.00		
7	06/12/10		Fliers		$22.45	
8	06/12/10		Paper and ink			$17.52
9						
10						

Even if Rusty does not record everything in his spreadsheet right away, he can always use the paper receipts to remember his expenses. He has his deposit slip to record his income. Rusty can use the receipt from Office Depot to record his expenses. Rusty keeps a box on his desk for paperwork that needs to be recorded into his spreadsheet.

Finally, after everything is recorded in his spreadsheet, Rusty files his deposit slips in a file folder labeled "Checking Account" and he files his Office Depot receipt in a file folder labeled Expenses.

What to Do Monthly

Every month you need to do several record keeping tasks for your micro business:

- **Record all your income.**

  Some micro businesses, such as babysitting, are always paid in cash. In these cases, keep an income ledger shown earlier or keep an envelope for your income. Then deposit all the cash from your business into your checking or savings account.

  If you want some cash for your personal use, resist taking it from your business income. Deposit your earnings first and then withdraw some cash for your personal use. (It is called an owner's draw.) Avoid the temptation to spend the cash you were just paid. Treat your business income deposit as a separate transaction from withdrawing cash for your personal use. This is to properly record your income for tax purposes. Do not mix business and personal spending.

- **Record all your expenses.** Categorize expenses by type of expense. Many business owners write the category of expense at the top of the receipt. I usually write BIZ across the top of receipts from office supply stores, so I can separate my business expenses from personal expenses.

- **Calculate your profit** by totaling the income and expense columns on your spreadsheet.

  Profit = Income — Expenses

Here's an example from Rusty's Dog Walking business

Rusty's Dog Walking and Biscuit Business
June

Date	Description	Income	Advertising	Office Supplies	Supplies	Inventory
06/08/10	Walked Jones dog	$8.00				
06/12/10	Johnson Pet Sitting	$25.00				
06/12/10	Walked Jones dog	$8.00				
06/12/10	Fliers		$22.45			
06/12/10	Paper and ink			$17.52		
06/15/10	Walked Jones dog	$8.00				
06/19/10	Walked Jones dog	$8.00				
06/22/10	Walked Jones dog	$8.00				
06/24/10	Extra leash				$12.00	
06/25/10	Sold 2 bags doggie treats	$12.00				
06/25/10	Walked Jones dog	$8.00				
06/25/10	Walked Peters dogs	$10.00				
06/29/10	Walked Jones dog	$8.00				
06/30/10	Talbot Pet Sitting	$45.00				
06/30/10	Purchase box of doggie treats					$36.00
Total		$148.00	$22.45	$17.52	$12.00	$36.00

- **Evaluate your progress.** How are you doing? Are you making a profit? Are you meeting your goals?

- **Pay anyone that you owe.** Keep a folder labeled "Accounts Payable/Bills to Pay." Accounts Payable is an accounting term that means people or businesses ("accounts") that you need to pay ("payable"). An example might be paying for a website.

- **Remind anyone that owes you** by sending them an email or a letter with an invoice. An invoice is a statement you send to your customers who still owe you money. Keep a folder labeled "Accounts Receivable" and store copies of invoices for which you have not received a payment. Rusty could make up an invoice and give it to the Johnsons and put a copy into his Accounts Receivable folder until he is paid.

- After you have recorded everything and added the totals, **carry the totals to a summary sheet** like the one shown below. This summary spreadsheet monitors the business performance every month. A quick glance reveals the major expenses and whether there is a profit, a loss, or break-even. This summary spreadsheet also makes tax preparation easy since all the expenses are summed by category.

Rusty's Dog Walking and Biscuit Business Summary					
Month	Income	Advertising	Office Supplies	Supplies	Inventory
January	$0.00				
February	$0.00				
March	$35.00				
April	$75.00	$12.00		$12.00	$36.00
May	$85.00	$0.00	$6.00	$0.00	$0.00
June	$148.00	$22.45	$17.52	$12.00	$36.00
July					
Total	$343.00	$34.45	$23.52	$24.00	$72.00

If you can, record your income and expenses on the same day they happen. Some micro business owners keep their bookkeeping records on their computer for quick updates or on a paper spreadsheet on their desk where it is always accessible. For others it is not convenient to record transactions every day. They create a "paper trail" and enter the transactions in their book at a later time.

> **Example:** Susie sells saddle blankets at horse shows. It is not convenient to enter her transactions every day, since she only goes to horse shows every few weeks. She creates a receipt for each sale and gives one copy to the customer and keeps a copy for herself. Susie bought a carbon-less receipt book for $4.00. She also keeps store receipts for her expenses such as fabric and records her mileage on a calendar in her cell phone. These three items are her "paper trail." She stores all her paperwork in an envelope and once a month sits down and records it all on a spreadsheet.

What to Do Quarterly

Every three months (once a quarter), you need to do several bookkeeping tasks for your micro business:

- Add up the previous three months' income and expenses. I recommend you do this for each quarter:
  - Quarter 1: January, February, and March
  - Quarter 2: April, May, and June
  - Quarter 3: July, August, and September
  - Quarter 4: October, November, and December.
- Pay taxes to the Internal Revenue Service (IRS) and your state. Ask for help from your accountant to calculate the taxes you owe. The next book in this series, *Money and Taxes in a Micro Business,* has de-

tails on understanding the federal and state taxes you may owe.

Here is a rough rule of thumb to follow:

If you have a profit of more than $500 in a quarter, it is time to meet with an accountant who can help estimate what you might owe in taxes.

Phil's mother called me and said, "Phillip is getting checks every month from Google for the ads on his website." I knew that Phil was paid when visitors clicked on Google-sponsored ads on his website. "What's the problem?" I asked. "The checks are for about $1,000 every month. I'm afraid he might owe some income tax," she explained. We set up an appointment that week to talk with Phillip about income, expenses, record keeping and estimated tax.

- Create a statement showing your income, expenses, and profit for the quarter.

- Evaluate your business. Are you doing better or worse than you planned? Where have you overspent your budget? Consider how you might make some changes. Predict your income and expenses for the next three months. You could call this your budget. Sometimes it is called a cash flow projection. It can be very helpful to see if you have enough cash on hand for your future plans.

Rusty's summary for each quarter is on the following page. He does not expect to pay any taxes this quarter according to my rule of thumb. (If you have a profit of more than $500 in a quarter, it is time to meet with an accountant who can help estimate what you might owe in taxes.)

Rusty's Dog Walking and Biscuit Business				
	Jan-March	April-June	July-Sept	Oct-Dec
Income	$35.00	$308.00		
Expenses	$0.00	$153.97		
Profit	$35.00	$154.03		
Estimated Tax				

Rusty takes time to evaluate his business. He is not showing as much profit as he would like at this point, so he is going to try harder to get more customers and sell more doggie treats. He also predicts that the next few months will have lower expenses. Overall, he is still on track to make $500 profit by the end of the year.

What to Do Annually

At the end of the year there are several bookkeeping tasks for your micro business. At the end of December, you will have monthly, quarterly, and annual tasks. If you have kept up with record keeping all year, this task will not take too much time. Do not wait until the end of the year to do your record keeping. It is too much work to do all at once.

One of my micro business clients was a woman who procrastinated about her record keeping. She always gave me her tax information late. I usually had to file for an extension of time because she would wait until June or later to gather her records for the previous year. By then, she had forgotten details and lost important documents. She probably paid more in taxes than she needed to because of her poor record keeping.

Do not be like my procrastinating tax client! Keeping up with your bookkeeping will give you a deeper understanding of your business and make tax preparation easier (and cheaper) for you and your accountant.

At the end of the year you should:

- Add up all four quarters of income and profit to get an annual amount.
- Create a statement showing your income and expenses.
- Calculate your profit and evaluate your progress. How did you do for the year? Did you meet your goals?
- Set up an appointment with your accountant for income tax preparation.
- Make up a budget for next year. What plans do you have? Do you have any ideas for expanding your business? Do you want to buy some equipment? Discuss your plans with your accountant.

Bookkeeping may seem overwhelming at first, but it is important in running a successful micro business. I covered what you will accomplish in an entire year, but you will do the bookkeeping in much smaller bits all year long. It will not be confusing once you get started. In the *Micro Business for Teens Workbook*, I offer a sample bookkeeping problem with answers. Working through the sample problem will give you enough experience and confidence to do your own bookkeeping.

Should You Learn Bookkeeping or Accounting?

Some micro business owners learn formal bookkeeping or accounting to help run their businesses better. A bookkeeping class will teach you how to correctly record business transactions. You could go beyond basic bookkeeping and take an accounting class where you will learn to create financial statements to help you make decisions in your business. If you continue to succeed in your business venture or pursue becoming a full-time entrepreneur, I highly recommend that you take at least one college-level accounting class. Known as the "language of business," accounting will teach you the correct terms and principles used in business to succeed.

Bookkeeping and Accounting Classes
Professor Michael Licata, PhD from Villanova University offers a Financial Accounting class, which is the first-year accounting class for business majors in college. Visit **www.ProfessorInABox.com** to learn more about this self-taught class.

If you want something a little less intense than a college-level accounting class, try a high school accounting class. Alpha Omega, a homeschool curriculum provider, offers high school-level accounting in a 10-workbook series **www.aophomeschooling.com/lifepac/electives/ accounting.**

The Potter's School (**www.pottersschool.org**) also offers on-line accounting classes for homeschool high school students.

Perhaps a full accounting class is not needed, but a simpler bookkeeping class might meet your immediate needs.

Bookkeeping is knowing how to record business transactions. Accountants take those transactions and create financial statements. One free on-line bookkeeping course is: **www.dwmbeancounter.com/tutorial/Tutorial.html**

You could also get some training in using the popular small business accounting software, QuickBooks. Many community colleges offer live or on-line classes in QuickBooks. Education To Go (**www.ed2go.com**) offers a six-week class, Introduction to QuickBooks.

Hire Help If You Need It

Perhaps you need some help right now and cannot take the time to learn bookkeeping. You might consider hiring a bookkeeper or an accountant.

What's the Difference Between a Bookkeeper and an Accountant?

Bookkeepers are people that record the daily transactions of a business. They pay the bills, balance the checking account, and mail out invoices (those are requests for payment from customers who haven't paid you yet). They usually have at least a high school degree and a few months of training in bookkeeping. On the other hand, accountants use the information from a bookkeeper to create reports, make a budget, file taxes and make decisions. Accountants have a four-year college degree.

Accountants can also do bookkeeping work, but it will probably be more expensive because accountants usually charge more per hour than a bookkeeper. The typical rate for a bookkeeper is $15-$30 per hour. An accountant may charge $50-$100 per hour.

When Should You Hire Outside Help?

I recommend you start your micro business and run it for at least six months, preferably a year, before you hire a bookkeeper. You want to be sure your business will be around for a while before you hire help, and you need to be sure you are making enough money to hire a bookkeeper. Additionally, you need to learn how to do basic bookkeeping yourself as a business owner before you hire someone to do it for you.

You should hire a bookkeeper when:
- you are too busy running your business to record your financial transactions *and*
- you can afford to pay a bookkeeper. They usually work on an hourly basis, and you might need a bookkeeper for one hour a week or more.

I recommend you hire a bookkeeper to help with record keeping that you cannot do yourself. For tax return preparation, however, hire an accountant, preferably a Certified Public Accountant (CPA).

Linda used me as her CPA for tax preparation and for business advice. She was doing all her own record keeping using QuickBooks, but found it was becoming very time-consuming. Linda needed to free up some time to focus on writing her next book, so she called me looking for a bookkeeper. We discussed her needs and she hired my daughter as her bookkeeper at $8.00/hour, much cheaper than my CPA rate of $50/hour. (By the way, bookkeeping is a great micro business for teenagers!)

What's a CPA?

A CPA is a certified public accountant who has studied accounting in college and has passed a grueling test, the CPA exam. CPAs have the ability to represent a business owner or individual before the Internal Revenue Service (IRS). They act as the ambassador between a taxpayer and the IRS.

A CPA is helpful to a micro business owner for many reasons. They provide:
- Tax returns
- Tax planning and estimates
- Advice on how to reduce taxes
- Advice on cash flow planning
- Help setting up a budget
- A review of your business plan

A good CPA can be a valuable advisor and resource for your business, even a micro business. Many will give you up to an hour of their time for no charge to meet you and discuss your business. Expect to pay $50-$100 an hour to call or meet with your CPA after the initial consultation. See my book *Money and Taxes in a Micro Business* for more information on how to work with an accountant and what they can do for you.

Important Points

- Create a simple bookkeeping system.
- Make a list of all your sources of income and expenses (called a Chart of Accounts).
- Record every transaction on paper or a spreadsheet.
- Sum the totals every month.
- Evaluate your progress every quarter.
- Compare your results at the end of the year with your plan.
- Make an appointment with your accountant to prepare your tax return.
- Consider taking a class in bookkeeping or accounting.
- Hire an accountant, preferably a CPA, for tax preparation.

Chapter Six
Using Software for Bookkeeping

As you start your micro business, there is so much to do and learn, including bookkeeping. It can be overwhelming. The easiest way to begin keeping your financial records is with a simple paper system, as I outlined in the previous chapter. Later, you may wish to keep records in an electronic spreadsheet. Eventually, you may want to use software to make data entry faster and easier. There are several good choices for micro business owners including, personal money management software programs or small business accounting programs.

Personal Money Management Software

Some micro business owners find that personal money management software such as Quicken, Mint.com, Moneydance, or GnuCash, can work very well for keeping their financial records. While not designed for small business purposes, these programs can certainly be a good start.

Personal money management software has these advantages:

- The program may already be loaded on your computer if your parents use it.
- Many online money management programs are free.
- They are very intuitive and look like a checkbook register.
- They can generate simple reports showing income and expenses.
- They can download checking account or Paypal information into your accounts.

Limitations of Personal Money Management Software

On the other hand, using personal money management software for business bookkeeping has some limitations.

- Cannot create invoices or send bills to your customers.
- Cannot create business financial statements, only transaction reports.
- Cannot record inventory.
- Cannot manage sales tax.

If you do use personal money management software I recommend the following practices:

- Create a separate account for your micro business. In other words, do not mix your business transactions in with your family's personal expenses and income.
- Change your settings to indicate that you will be running a business. Many software packages will create categories that relate to running a business.
- Many of the software providers offer several variations.

For example, Quicken offers a Starter edition, as well as Deluxe, Premier, and Home & Businesses editions that offer more features.

- The free programs such as Mint.com have ads and opportunities to purchase financial products such as loans. Try not to be distracted by them.
- Many people have concerns about putting their financial information on-line, so ask your parents' permission before using an on-line program.

Learning to Use Personal Money Management Software
Most software packages come with several video tutorials such as setup, managing your bills, and paying bills. These are quite short, but should be enough to get you started.

The website **www.lynda.com** sells a video on Quicken. You can watch it online or purchase it.

YouTube has several short tutorials on Quicken, Mint, and Moneydance. As with anything on YouTube, the quality varies. Some videos can be quite good, while others are difficult to see or hear.

Small Business Accounting Software

There are some micro businesses that could benefit from using small business accounting software. If you need to send invoices, want better reporting, or have inventory, then you will need to consider software for small business accounting such as QuickBooks, Peachtree, or MYOB. Here's what accounting software can do for you:

- Print checks, pay bills, track sales and expenses
- Reconcile bank accounts
- Create estimates, invoices and reports

- Compute payroll and track employee time
- Create financial reports showing income, expenses and profit (or loss)
- Download credit card and bank transactions
- Track inventory and set reorder points
- Create business plans, budgets, and forecasts

The features of accounting software can vary by provider and the version. Obviously, the more you pay for the software, the more features you receive. QuickBooks comes in several variations including Mac and PC versions, an on-line version and software for single or multiple users. Quick-Books Pro is a popular version and a good place to start. It typically sells for around $200. You can view a comparison chart of the various QuickBooks versions at **Quickbooks.intuit.com.**

Limitations of Accounting Software
- Accounting software is more difficult to learn than personal money management software. It may involve time reading, taking a class, or getting professional assistance to set up the accounts correctly.
- Accounting software is more expensive than personal finance software. Typical prices begin around $200.
- Many times, the software provider discontinues support and downloads from your bank after three years and you must purchase an update.
- The software must be used in the way it was designed. For example, if you record a deposit before you record the sale, your sales records will not be correct. This can become a tangled mess to sort out at tax time.

Learning Accounting Software

The most popular small business accounting software is QuickBooks and so there are many ways to learn how to use it.

Several community colleges offer training in accounting software. Some are classes with live instructors while some classes are offered online. Visit **www.Ed2Go.com**, the provider of many online classes for community colleges, to find classes in QuickBooks and Peachtree near you or on-line.

The website **www.lynda.com** has a video on QuickBooks. You can watch it on-line or purchase it.

Professional help is available. Intuit, the maker of Quick-Books, has a program called QuickBooks ProAdvisor to help users find local certified professionals. See **Proadvisor.intuit.com/referral.** These QuickBooks professionals can set up the software, train you, and troubleshoot problems.

A Free Alternative

A small business accounting package called GnuCash is open source software that is available for no charge. Open source software is available free of charge as an alternative to commercial software programs. The source code is open and can be shared, viewed, and modified by other users and programmers. As with many open source programs, the training is sparse. Expect to do a lot of learning on your own. Visit **GnuCash.org** to download the program.

Recommendation

I recommend that you start your micro business with keeping records on paper or in a computer spreadsheet for at least three months. This gives you time to know what your sources of income and expenses will be. If you find you are using more than four or five categories of expenses, consider using a spreadsheet with a separate column for each expense.

You might want to move your record keeping into a personal money management program after a few months. This may be all you ever need to run your business. But if you find you need to send invoices to customers or you sell products and carry inventory, you should look into using accounting software.

If you want to use small business accounting software, try QuickBooks Pro or GnuCash.

If you buy and sell inventory, buy QuickBooks Pro and devote time or money to learning how to use it. You could save a little money and buy last year's version. The current version sells for about $200.

My Personal Progression

In the beginning of my accounting business, I recorded my income and expenses on paper for three years. I used a columnar pad that I bought for $1.99 at an office supply store. I summarized the paper records into my personal finance software, Quicken, and had two general categories: "Carol's Business Income" and "Business Expense." At that time all my income was from preparing tax returns which were paid on delivery, so I never had to send an invoice to a client and I had no inventory. Record keeping was simple.

After five years, I grew to add a few small business clients that needed to be billed or were paying in installments, so I switched to QuickBooks Pro so that I could prepare and track invoices. Now I have inventory (books), sales tax (on my book sales), and I invoice more clients. QuickBooks is now indispensable to me.

Important Points

- Record keeping can be made easier by using software programs.

- Some micro businesses find using personal money management software works well for them.

- Small business accounting software such as Quick-Books may be needed if you sell inventory or want to send invoices to clients.

- There are several methods to learn accounting software programs.

Chapter Seven
Legal Names and Numbers

Since a hobby can turn into a profitable micro business, some teenagers find themselves in business quite by accident. The book *Lawn Boy*, by children's author Gary Paulsen, is a funny story about how he found himself in business as a 12-year-old boy who had been given an old riding lawn mower to "tinker with."

> *The front lawn didn't take too long, but before I was done the next-door neighbor came to the fence, attracted by the cloud of dust. He waved me over.*
>
> *"You mow lawns?" he asked, "How much?"*
>
> *And that was how it started.*

If you find yourself in business, whether planned or unintended, there are probably a lot of questions that you have. Some of the most pressing questions may be about what you should call business and what legal issues you may encounter in running a micro business. When running a business, even a small one, there are names to consider and numbers to obtain, such as an Employer Identification Number (EIN) with the Internal Revenue Service.

This chapter will answer some questions about names and numbers that you may have such as:

- Does a micro business need a name?
- When is a business license needed?
- Should a micro business be a sole proprietorship or consider partners?
- When is a tax ID number needed?

Does a Micro Business Need a Name?

Many teenage micro businesses do not need a separate business name; they can just use the owner's name. I recommend that micro business owners delay using a business name until they know if the business will last and be profitable. Business names cost money, so you do not want to spend your hard-earned profits on a business name if your business may close down in a short time.

Instead of creating a business name, consider using a tag line on your business cards and advertising. For example, you could say something like "Emma Thomas, piano teacher to your little Mozart." The business's legal name is Emma Thomas, and the tag line explains what Emma does.

If you really want a business name, you will need to register your name with your state or local government. This registration is called a "doing business as" (or DBA) name registration. The government office you need to contact depends on the local laws in your area. In my state of Ohio, the form is called a "Fictitious Name Registration" and it costs $50.

Consider your name carefully and do some research before picking a name. You cannot use some words such as "Inc.," "Co." or "LLC," because those titles are reserved for certain types of corporations and companies.

The web is a great place to do a name search, especially if you will have a website for your business. The site Whols.com can tell you what website names are available, but that is not the same as a legal business name registration.

To determine if your favorite name is available, you need to do a name search at your Secretary of State's website. Google your state and "Secretary of State." Then search around for a listing of businesses registered in your state.

If you are unsure about your local or state rules concerning business names, visit **www.business.gov/ register/business-name/ dba.html** for lists of the requirements for filing a fictitious business name in each state.

For many years, I ran my accounting practice as simply Carol Topp, CPA. It was easy. I used my real name on my business card and checking account. No fictitious name or DBA registration was needed. Then I created a website and called it HomeschoolCPA. I registered that name with Ohio's Secretary of State. It required one page to fill out and cost me $50. Now no one else can be called HomeschoolCPA in Ohio.

When Is a Business License Needed?

Like creating a name for your business, obtaining a business license depends on where you live. There are federal, state, and local requirements that dictate when a business owner needs a license.

Federal License
Let's start at the top with the United States federal license. If you are in any of the following types of businesses, you will need a federal license:

Agriculture, alcohol, aviation, firearms and explosives, fish & wildlife, maritime transportation, mining & drilling, nuclear energy, and radio and TV production.

These businesses are beyond the scope of almost all micro businesses, and especially teenage micro businesses. (You're not creating nuclear energy in your basement, are you?) Therefore, so it is probably safe to assume that you will not need a federal license to operate your micro business in the United States.

State Professional License
At the state level, many professions are required to have a license. Common examples include:

accountants   beauticians

lawyers   architects

doctors   barbers

electricians   insurance agents

Most teenagers are not eligible for these professions because of their age and level of education, so again, it is unlikely that most teenage-owned micro businesses will be granted a professional license.

A helpful site from the US government will link you to your state's licensing requirements: **www.business.gov/ register/licenses-and-permits.**

Local Permits and Licenses
At the local level, the city and/or county requirements for businesses vary widely. Common business permits and licenses include:

- Vendor's license if you sell products
- Health permits, especially if you sell food for human consumption.
- Building, zoning, sign, and occupancy permits

The website listed above (**www.business.gov/register/ licenses-and-permits**) lets you input your zip code and business type and will then direct you to a website with specific information. Examples of business types include auto dealership, barber shop, and childcare services. If you are unsure of how to classify your business, just pick general business. You will be linked to your local city or county website.

Some local or county websites are easier to navigate than others. If you cannot find what your local requirements are, call your local government office and ask about business licenses. They will explain local zoning and occupancy requirements, especially if you have a home office. For example, my local government has restrictions on how much space I can use for a business in my home and how many cars may park outside my house on a regular basis.

Should a Micro Business Be a Sole Proprietorship?

Most books about starting a small business start with a chapter on deciding your business type. The major types of business structures in the United States today are:

- Sole proprietorships which have only one owner
- Partnerships which have more than one owner
- Corporations which are owned by many owners called shareholders

Frequently, business guides tell you that making a decision about your business entity is a serious decision and must be made before you begin your business. You are told to do extensive reading and are advised to consult a lawyer. It can often stop you in your tracks even before you get started!

These guides are well intended, but are overkill for micro businesses. I recommend that a micro business be formed as a sole proprietorship and you should not be concerned with forming partnerships or corporations.

Advantages of sole proprietorships include:

- Sole proprietorships are quicker and easy to start

- No partnership agreements are needed.

- No corporation status is needed. Corporations are complex to set up, including filing forms with the Secretary of State, paying a filing fee, and abiding by annual reporting requirements.

- Sole proprietorships are easier to close. Partnerships and corporations are sometimes very complex to close down. A sole proprietorship closes down when the owner decides he wants to move on.

- Sole proprietorship businesses are easy to understand. Partnerships and corporations usually need a lawyer to draft contracts with legal language that is difficult to understand.

- Has the simplest tax structure. A sole proprietorship uses a two-page tax form (Schedule C Business Income or Loss) and attaches it to his or her personal tax return. Partnerships and corporations, however, require completely separate multi-page tax returns and additional forms added to the owners' individual tax returns.

- No lawyer is needed. Legal advice might be a good idea if you are signing a lease or applying for a patent, but most micros work from home and never invent anything new, so they can operate for years without needing a lawyer. However, if you form a partnership or corporation, you should hire an attorney to advise you.

- You keep the profits. Partnerships and corporations distribute their profits to partners or shareholders. The owner of a sole proprietorship keeps all the profits.

- You have no investors to keep happy. You, the micro business owner, need to be happy with your business' progress, not outside investors or partners.

Should a Teenager Start a Business With a Friend?

Some teenagers like the idea of starting a micro business with a friend. After all, it is more fun to do things with a friend who can help and encourage you. However, I discourage micro business owners from starting a business with a partner. There can be a lot of problems (and emotions) involved with working with other people. Partnerships are permanent, both legally and financially. They are like being married to another person because they are difficult to break! In *Starting a Micro Business,* I discussed the problems with partnerships. For now, start your business as the sole owner. If you need help, ask a friend to assist you in your business, but make it clear that you are the only owner.

When Is a Tax ID Number Needed?

If you make a profit in your micro business, there is a good chance that you will owe taxes. In *Money and Taxes in a Micro Business,* I discuss the details of how much you might pay in taxes. But first, you need to know about a tax ID number.

A sole proprietor does not need a special tax ID number. He or she can simply use a Social Security Number (SSN) as their ID number on their tax forms.

While you may use your SSN to operate a sole proprietorship, many small business owners use a business tax ID number called an EIN (Employer Identification Number). An EIN is similar to a Social Security Number but it is for businesses. You can obtain an EIN from the Internal Revenue Service (IRS) for no charge. Go to **www.irs.gov/taxtopics/tc755.html** for more information on the EIN.

Why Would a Micro Business Want an EIN?

A sole proprietorship may want an EIN for:

- Privacy. Using an EIN protects your SSN. Many small business owners are concerned about identity theft and so they get and use an EIN and keep their SSN private.
- Opening a bank account. Many banks want an EIN to open a business checking account.
- The IRS requires it for hiring employees, forming a corporation, partnership or limited liability company.

You do not need to have a business name to apply for an EIN. You can simple obtain an EIN using your personal name. My EIN is in my name as "Carol L. Topp CPA." The IRS allows a person to use one EIN for all the businesses a sole proprietorship might own. So you can use your EIN for as many micro businesses as you start. You can even change the name of your business and keep your old EIN.

How to Obtain an EIN from the IRS

To get your EIN go to **www.irs.gov** and search for "EIN." You can fill in the SS-4 on-line or print it out for mailing. Keep a copy for yourself. If you are in a hurry, you can also apply for an EIN by telephone (800-829-4933), fax, or on-line.

Here's a short video the IRS made explaining EINs for small businesses:
www.tax.gov/SmallBusinessTaxpayer/StartingaBusiness/EIN.

Important Points

- Many micro businesses do not use a business name. They just use the owner's name.

- If you choose to use a business name, you must register it with your state or local government.

- Business licenses may be required for specific industries and professions.

- Local laws may require a vendor's license, food safety license, or building and zoning permits.

- Sole proprietorships have many advantages for a micro business over partnerships or corporations.

- A sole proprietorship may use the owner's Social Security Number and does not need an Employer Identification Number (EIN).

- Some sole proprietorships may prefer to use an EIN for privacy or for banking purposes.

Chapter Eight
Reducing Risk

Is Insurance Needed for a Micro Business?

Most businesses need insurance to protect them in case of a disaster, but does a micro business need insurance? The answer depends on what your business makes or sells, your amount of risk, and the type of insurance. Although there are dozens of insurance policies a business could purchase, most do not apply to teenage-owned businesses. For example, teenagers rarely need life, disability or key person insurance because they do not have dependents relying on their income. All these policies pay your dependents (called beneficiaries) if you die. If no one depends upon you for money, these insurance policies are unnecessary. Likewise, most teenagers are covered under their parents' health insurance, so the business does not need to buy health insurance.

Here is a list of very common business insurance policies and cases when they might be needed by a teenage micro business owner:

Type of Insurance	Explanation	Needed by a teenage business owner?	Notes
General Liability	The most common type of business insurance. Covers lawsuits, injury claims, property loss	maybe	If the policy is not expensive and your micro business has some elements of risk, this might be worthwhile
Health	covers doctor and hospital bills	no	Teenagers are typically covered under family health insurance
Life	pays a loved one if you die	no	No one depends on the teenager's income
Disability	pays you if you become disabled	no	No one depends on the teenager's income
Key Person Insurance	pays your company if you (as the key person) dies	no	No one depends on the teenager's income
Home-based Business	Will cover your business property, records, and some of your income in case of disaster	maybe	Most home owners policies do not cover a home business
Internet Business	Covers damage from viruses or hackers or data loss	maybe	Could be helpful if your website generates income.
Malpractice	Covers professionals like doctors who might be sued	no	teenagers are not usually professionals
Property	covers losses to your business property from fire, rain, floods, etc.	maybe	Recommended if the business has expensive equipment or inventory
Product Liability	pays for lawsuits where someone was injured using your product or service	maybe	Needed if the product you sell could injure someone
Business Interruption	Pays if your business is interrupted for a period of time due to flood, fire or disaster	rarely	No one is depending on the teenager's income to live on

As you can see from the chart, only a few types of insurance could be needed by a teenage micro business owner. The general liability policy or the home-based business policy might be the first types of insurance to consider.

Home-based Business Insurance

Nolo.com, a legal information website, has some good reasons why a home-based business insurance policy might be helpful.

> Do not rely exclusively on your regular homeowners' or renters' policy to protect your home business, at least without checking first with the insurance company. Many of these policies do not cover business use of a home, which means that you probably won't be protected against losses relating to your business. For example:
>
> - After your computer is stolen, you may find out that it's not covered by your homeowner's policy because business property is excluded.
>
> - After your house burns down, you may find that your fire coverage is void because you didn't tell the insurance company that you were using your home for business.
>
> - After a delivery person slips on your front porch and breaks his leg, you may find that you're not covered for injuries associated with business deliveries.
>
> It's easy to avoid these nasty surprises. Sit down with your insurance agent and fully disclose your planned business operations. It's relatively inexpensive to add riders to your homeowner's policy to cover normal business risks. [1]

[1] http://www.nolo.com/legal-encyclopedia/article-29943.html,

As the Nolo.com article points out, insurance for your micro business can be added onto your parents' homeowners policy (called a rider). If you close the business, have your parents cancel that part of the policy. You should pay your parents for the additional cost to insure your business and it can be deducted on your micro business tax return as a business expense.

When to Consider Business Insurance

As in many situations, I recommend making a decision after your business has been in operation for about a year and you think it will continue for another year. Alternatively, there are some high-risk businesses that need insurance coverage as soon as they begin, such as horseback riding lessons. Talk to your parents about the need for insurance. Then, with them, call or visit their insurance agent. Ask about home-based business insurance, what it covers, and what it costs.

What Is an LLC?

The American tax system offers three choices for a business structure:

- sole proprietorships, which have only one owner
- partnerships, which have two or more owners and
- Corporations, which have several owners called shareholders

I usually recommend that a teenage micro business owner not be overly concerned about choosing a business structure. The sole proprietorship is the easiest and quickest way to start a micro business. I advise teenagers to avoid partnerships and find that corporations are overly complex for a micro business. However, there is a business term that you may have heard about called LLC or Limited Liability Company. Some of my teenage business clients have formed their micro businesses as LLCs.

LLC stands for Limited Liability Company. It is a legal status for your business that provides you, the owner, with legal protection called limited liability.

An LLC can have many owners (called members), but I recommend that micro businesses stay with only one owner, so a single-member LLC is the type I would suggest. A single-member LLC is just like a sole proprietorship in its operations and tax status, but it has the added benefit of limited liability.

What is Limited Liability?

Owners (called members) of an LLC are not personally liable for the LLC's debts and obligations. That means if someone sues your business, they can take the LLC's assets, but cannot touch your personal assets. An asset is anything you own such as a car, house or money in the bank. The owner's liability is limited to the assets of the LLC, such as your business checking account, your inventory, or your business computer. The person suing you cannot touch your college savings account, because the liability is limited to the business' money, not your personal money.

Does Being an LLC Save On Taxes?

Being an LLC does not alter your business structure in the eyes of the IRS. The IRS has only three classifications of for-profit businesses: sole proprietorship, partnership, or corporation. In the past, limited liability was only available to corporations, but in the 1980s, LLCs became very popular and available in every state. Now, sole proprietorships can have limited liability without becoming a corporation.

Single member LLCs still file the same tax return as sole proprietors, the Schedule C Business Profit or Loss. If you called the IRS and asked, "What tax form does an LLC use?" they would ask if you are a sole proprietorship, partnership, or corporation. The IRS does not recognize LLCs. Certainly they know LLCs exist, but the IRS calls LLCs "disregarded entities," meaning that, for tax purposes, having LLC status does not change anything. LLC is a legal status, not a tax status.

Why Would a Sole Proprietor Need Limited Liability?
Limited liability protects your personal assets such as a house or college savings from lawsuits arising from your business. If your business involves any significant risk or if you hire employees, there is some risk of being sued.

Risks might include:
- personal services that can cause injury or harm, such as a personal trainer
- giving advice or consulting
- food preparation and sales
- caring for children
- product sales which could potentially cause injury or harm
- hiring employees

Existence of these risks means that LLC status could be an option for your business. Child care is on the list above, but I do not mean to imply that a teenage babysitter needs to file for limited liability status. What I am recommending is that you know about LLC status and its benefits so that if your micro business grows into a full-fledged child care operation you might consider obtaining limited liability.

As a general guideline, I think that most micro businesses could be in operation up to a year before the owner considers obtaining LLC status. Obviously, the need for limited liability depends on the nature and size of your business.

Lucas was 17 when he filed for LLC status for his lawn care micro business. He had several reasons for doing so. First, he had been running the business for two years and knew he would keep it going for a while. He had hired three friends as employees to help him when he needed it. He was also in a risky business, mowing lawns around customers' houses where accidents can happen. Finally, he had made a healthy profit over the years and wanted to protect his savings account. These are all excellent reasons to form an LLC. Lucas' business is still a sole proprietorship and forming an LLC did not change what he paid in taxes, but it gave him and his parents some peace of mind.

How to Obtain LLC Status

You must file a request with your state government to become an LLC. Usually, the Secretary of State's (SOS) office has a website that explains what forms to use and the fees involved. Do a Google search on your state and "Secretary of State." At the SOS's website there is usually information about starting a business and filing forms to be an LLC. There is usually a fee involved and it can vary from $50 to $500 depending on your state.

While learning about LLCs from your Secretary of State's

website, make note of any other requirements your state might impose. For example, in Tennessee, LLCs must file an annual report and pay an annual fee in addition to the initial $300 filing fee.

Is a Lawyer Needed to Form an LLC?
If you are unsure if you want to become and LLC or are confused by the terms on the forms from your Secretary of State, it is time to talk to a lawyer. Perhaps your micro business is not ready for LLC status yet, so find a lawyer who might consult with you for free for half an hour. They can guide you to know when and if LLC status is right for you.

Important Points

- There are many types of insurance a business own-er may consider.

- Several types of insurance are not needed by a teenage micro business owner with no dependents.

- Consider home-based business insurance as a rid-er to your parents' homeowner policy.

- Liability can be limited to only business assets with Limited Liability Company status.

- LLC is a legal status, not a tax status, and does change your tax liability.

- High risk businesses might benefit from LLC status.

Chapter Nine
Time Management

If you are a typical teenage micro business owner, you are most likely a busy person. Micro business owners juggle running a business with homework, time with family, and with friends. Some are active in sports, clubs, church activities, and scouts. It is possible to run a micro business and do many other activities in life, but it takes good time management skills.

In this chapter, I will discuss the importance of setting goals so you do not waste time. You will also complete a survey of where you spend your time now so you can see opportunities to improve. Additionally, I share tips to getting a lot done in a little bit of time.

If you aim at nothing, you'll hit it every time.
Zig Ziglar, motivational author

Goal Setting

People who accomplish a lot usually have specific goals. They usually do not waste time because their goal strongly motivates them to use their time well.

As a micro business owner, you have dreams, such as making money or learning something new. You may have a large ambition and to achieve it you may need to break a large goal into smaller steps.

> Todd wanted to buy a used car by his 16th birthday. He needed $3,000 and started to work very hard over the summer in his lawn mowing micro business. He was motivated to mow a lot of grass because the summer mowing season doesn't last very long and he had a large goal.

1. Define your goal. What do you want to see happen? This can be a big goal such as "earn $10,000 for a car," or something smaller, such as "set up a website for my micro business."

2. Break your target down into smaller steps. Obviously, the larger the goal, the more steps it will take to attain it. For example, to earn $10,000 might start with launching a micro business now, expanding it over the next year, and having the money within two years.

3. Consider possible roadblocks and ways to overcome them. There will be challenges along your path to success and if you can foresee them now, they will be easier to overcome. With planning and foresight, these bumps in the road will be only small problems

to manage, not complete roadblocks that force you to give up.

Consider this roadblock: You need a website but do not have the knowledge to create one. This is a difficulty, but not a reason to give up. Instead of quitting, plan how you will overcome the problem. Perhaps you could ask a friend who has created a website to tell you how they learned, or try a Google search to learn more.

4. Set deadlines. When do you want to achieve your goal? Can it be accomplished in a week or will you need a month? Be reasonable so you do not put too much pressure on yourself.

SMART Goals
The acronym, SMART, helps in the goal-setting process.

Specific. A goal should be specific enough to answer the question: What do you want to accomplish? An example of a specific goal is: I want to increase my list of Facebook fans. An unspecific goal would be vague such as, "I need to advertise my business."

Measurable. A goal should be measured in some way. Think about how much or how many when you set a goal. For example, a measurable goal might be to increase your email list to 100 names.

Action oriented. A goal needs to have an action associated with it. Ask yourself, "How will I accomplish my goal? List a few verbs or action words such as gather, invite, email, call, etc. To continue the email list example, an action-oriented goal might be to add an email sign up box on the homepage of your website.

Reasonable. A SMART goal is something you can reasonably attain. Ask yourself, "Can I reasonably do this?" For example, it is not reasonable for me to think I will ever play professional basketball since I am only a little over 5 feet tall, but perhaps I could aim for improving my shooting average. That would be a reasonable goal for me.

Timely. SMART goals have a time limit. When will you be able to reach this goal? How long will it take? Adding 100 new names to an email list might take a month or two.

A chart can be helpful in setting goals. Start with listing some specific goals in measurable terms (the S and M parts of SMART). Then write down action steps and a finish date (the A and T portions of a SMART goal). Finally, consider any obstacles you might encounter so it stays reasonable and who could assist you in finding a solution.

Goal (SM)	Action Steps (A)	Obstacles(R)	Finish Date (T)	Who Can Help

An example might be helpful. A teenager has a goal to make $500 by the end of the summer, August 30. She determines she can teach five piano students and reach her goal. She breaks down her big goal into several smaller goals.

Goal (SM)	Action Steps (A)	Obstacles(R)	Finish Date (T)	Who Can Help
Make $500 this summer	Teach piano lessons for 10 weeks to 5 students	Finding students	Aug 30	Mom
Find 5 piano students	Make up fliers and an email		May 30	Mom
Send out email to 5 places	email church friends, email babysitter clients	need more people to email!	May 15	Little sister, her friends, mom
Decide on price and piano books to use	Do a mini market survey to find what piano teachers charge	find piano teachers or piano students to ask	May 15	friends taking piano lessons
Make a business plan	Read Starting a Micro Business	Just do it!	May 1	

To Do Lists

I recommend that you keep breaking down your goals until they are in small segments that can be accomplished in one to two hours. Your list may become quite long, but don't get discouraged. Planning the tasks that need to be done is a huge step toward accomplishing them. Even Jesus saw the advantage in planning ahead.

Suppose one of you wants to build a tower. Will he not first sit down and estimate the cost to see if he has enough money to complete it?

Jesus in Luke 4:28

If you have a lot of tasks to accomplish, it helps to prioritize them. You can mark each item as high, medium, or low priority. I like to use highlighters of different colors. Yellow is high priority, pink is medium, and blue is low priority. Focus on the high priority items that can be done in a short amount of time, like a week. Do those first. Cross them off when they are accomplished. This gives you a visual reminder of your goals and can be a great motivator as you see more things crossed off your list.

Some people re-write their task lists every week or even every day, if the list is short. I write up a To Do list by priority every month and then have a very short list of what I want to accomplish every week. You can work out a system that is best for you. By the way, this system of keeping a To Do list works great to manage your homework assignments too!

My father makes a list of what he needs to do every day. He has a goal of keeping a nice yard, so his list includes weeding, fertilizing the grass, planting flowers, etc. He's retired, so sometimes his list says "take a nap"! He likes being able to cross off items as he does them and it gives him a sense of accomplishment.

Time Management

Before you can begin to work on time management, you should be aware of where you are spending your time now. Thefollowing chart should be filled in as you go about your day. You could rely on your memory, but it is best to look at the clock and write down what you are doing as you go through your day.

Daily Schedule

Time	Monday	Tuesday	Wednesday	Thursday	Friday	Saturday	Sunday
6:00 AM							
7:00 AM							
8:00 AM							
9:00 AM							
10:00 AM							
11:00 AM							
12:00 PM							
1:00 PM							
2:00 PM							
3:00 PM							
4:00 PM							
5:00 PM							
6:00 PM							
7:00 PM							
8:00 PM							
9:00 PM							
10:00 PM							
11:00 PM							
12:00 AM							

After you have filled in the chart, circle any times that are blank or times that you wasted. Try to define what wasted time is to you. Some teenagers might have playing video games on their schedule. Is that wasted time? Maybe, but to some people, videos are entertaining and relaxing. If one of your goals is to launch a website, you might consider limiting your game time until the goal is reached.

What did you see about yourself? Is there anything you want to change?

Failing to plan is planning to fail.
Alan Lakein, author of time management books

Schedule Your Time
Next, you should make up a schedule that will be a plan of your week. Take a clean copy of the chart above and fill it in with what you want your schedule to look like. Try not to schedule every minute. The hour-long blocks that I use on the chart are specific enough. You may not stick to it perfectly, but try to have a general schedule.

Here are some tips for creating a weekly schedule:

- Be flexible. Don't schedule every minute. Leave some time blank for flexibility, fun, and relaxation.
- Do not forget to leave time for showering, getting dressed, etc. It takes more time than you may think, especially if you are a teenage girl!
- Schedule time for your family. Leave room for an after-school chat with your parents or a family dinner.
- Allow time for driving. If soccer practice starts at 4:00 p.m. and it takes 20 minutes to drive there, mark soccer practice as starting at 3:30 p.m.

- Allow enough time to sleep. Studies have shown that teenagers need more sleep than children, but most do not get enough.

What If You Cannot Get It All Done?

Sometimes the work and activities pile up and you cannot do everything as you planned. What do you do then? Try not to panic; it might cause you to shut down and not accomplish anything!

- Prioritize your activities. Write up a new To Do list and look at what you have as high priorities. Maybe they can be moved to a lower priority level and take some pressure off yourself.

> Emily was writing her resume, but she had no plans to need one for several months. She had it on her To Do list for a particular week, but since it was a low priority, she could move it to the following week when she became too busy.

- Cancel or quit some activities. You may have to cancel a few clients or skip an activity once in a while to manage your time more efficiently.

Therefore be careful how you walk (or live), not as unwise men, but as wise, making the most of your time.
The Bible, book of Ephesians 5:15-16a

- Ask for help at home. See if a sibling can do some of your chores. Offer to pay them. It might cost you a few dollars, but your time and sanity are worth it.

- Ask yourself, "Is this really important?" You may decide it is not urgent and can be put off a few days or weeks. Focus on what is important and lasting to you. Do not neglect family and friends for the sake of making money.

Whoever loves money never has enough; whoever loves wealth is never satisfied with his income.
The Bible, book of Ecclesiastes 5:10

- Ask yourself, "Who has set the deadline—you or another person?" If you have imposed a deadline, perhaps it can be moved. I create a lot of self-imposed deadlines. I found myself complaining to my husband that I was not releasing a book as quickly as I had hoped. "Who made up that deadline?" he asked me. I had to admit that I had, and I was free to move it back if needed. No one suffered and I was free from a lot of stress.

- Cut down on TV, emails, and surfing the internet. My daughter, Sarah, went on a Facebook fast for a week when homework and others things were really piling up. She had seen other friends avoid Facebook for a week and knew that she could do it too. She was happy to prove she had the discipline to forego her social networking time and was pleased that she got a lot of schoolwork done that week!

Hiring Help

In general, I discourage micro business owners from hiring employees. Employees bring a lot of extra paperwork and taxes that you, as a teenage business owner, do not need. Wait until you have more business experience, at least two or three years, before you hire an employee.

Instead of hiring employees, I recommend finding another micro business owner that you can hire to do a specific project. (They would be called an *independent contractor.*) In writing this book, I hired several independent contractors:

- A graphic designer to create the book cover
- An editor to read over the book and correct my mistakes
- A website designer to build a website
- A virtual assistant to set up a shopping cart on my website.

None of these people are my employees. They are independent contractors (IC) hired for a specific task. The paperwork is minimal and there are no taxes to pay when hiring an IC. They were all micro business owners, and some of them were teenagers!

Learning More About Independent Contractors

In my book, *Money and Taxes in a Micro Business*, I discuss hiring employees (if you must) and paying independent contractors in detail. You should know a few things now about hiring independent contractors.

1. If you pay any independent contractor more than $600 a year, you will need to file a tax form called a 1099MISC and send it to the worker and to the IRS.

2. Collect the independent contractor's legal name, address and Social Security Number.

3. Agree on the price for the job before the worker begins. Pay a bit at the start and the remainder when he or she finishes the job. Try to avoid paying everything up front. (I learned that the hard way!)

4. Get a few recommendations before you hire someone, especially if the IC has been hired on-line and you have never met him or her in person.

5. Get a phone number from the independent contractor, not just an email address. Call him or her before you agree to work together and before you send the first payment. (I learned that the hard way too!)

This may sound like a lot to do when hiring an independent contractor, but hiring an employee is even more involved! Hiring employees involves more paperwork and paying employer taxes, such as Social Security, Medicare, worker's compensation, and unemployment insurance.

Encourage Another Micro Business Owner

If you are overloaded with work, but do not want to hire an employee, encourage another teenager to take over some of your workload and start their own micro business.

No one can do it all and you will hurt yourself by trying. If there is too much business for you to do, both you and your customers will suffer. Instead, encourage a friend to start their own business. Help them out by giving them a few of your clients, so your life is more manageable.

Important Points

- Getting it all done begins with setting goals.
- SMART goals are specific, measurable, action-oriented, reasonable, and timely.
- A To Do list can be helpful for managing your goals.
- Time management begins with taking a survey of where you currently spend your time.
- A weekly schedule can help you manage your time better.
- If you cannot get it all done, you may need to change your priorities or activities.
- You may need to hire help as an independent contractor to accomplish some tasks.

About the Author

Carol Topp, CPA, owner of **www.CarolToppCPA.com** and **MicroBusinessForTeens.com,** helps people, especially teenagers, start their own small businesses.

Carol was born and raised in Racine, Wisconsin and graduated from Purdue University with a degree in engineering. She worked ten years for the US Navy as a cost analyst before staying home with her two daughters. While being a stay-at-home mom, Carol took accounting classes via distance learning. In 2000, Carol received her CPA license and opened her own practice.

She is a member of the Ohio Society of CPAs, the National Association of Tax Professionals, and the Society of Nonprofit Organizations. Carol has presented numerous workshops on money management, business start up, taxes, budgeting, and homeschooling to various community, church, and homeschool groups.

She has authored several books including:

- *Homeschool Co-ops: How to Start Them, Run Them and Not Burn Out*
- *Information in a Nutshell: Business Tips and Taxes for Writers*
- *Teens and Taxes: A Guide for Parents and Teenagers*

And several magazine articles in:

- *The Old Schoolhouse*
- *Home Education*
- *Homeschool Enrichment*
- National Association of Tax Professionals *TaxPro*
- *Nonprofit World*

Carol lives in Cincinnati, Ohio with her husband and two daughters where she runs her micro business from her home.

If you enjoyed *Running a Micro Business,* look for the next two books in the Micro Business for Teens series.

Starting a Micro Business covers the characteristics of a micro business, ideas, creating a business plan, starting with no debt, and staying motivated.

Money and Taxes in a Micro Business covers financial statements, income taxes, tax deductions, sales tax, employees, and working with an accountant.

Micro Business for Teens Workbook is designed for individual or group study. Put into practice what you read in *Starting a Micro Business* and *Running a Micro Business.*

Also available are audios, webinars, and videos on starting and running a micro business.

Available at **MicroBusinessForTeens.com**

Made in the USA
Middletown, DE
18 September 2017